CLASSIC RIVALRIES

CLASSIC RIVALRIES

The Most Memorable Matchups in Sports History

INTRODUCTION BY JACK McCALLUM

TEXT BY HANK HERSCH AND MARK BECHTEL

TIME INC. HOME ENTERTAINMENT
President . . . . Rob Gursha
Vice President, Branded Businesses . . . . David Arfine
Vice President, New Product Development . . . . Richard Fraiman
Executive Director, Marketing Services . . . . Carol Pittard
Director, Retail & Special Sales . . . . Tom Mifsud
Director of Finance . . . . Tricia Griffin
Brand Manager . . . . Niki Whelan
Prepress Manager . . . . Emily Rabin
Associate Book Production Manager . . . . Suzanne Janso
Associate Product Manager . . . . Victoria Alfonso

special thanks to:
Bozena Bannett, Robert Dente, Gina Di Meglio, Anne-Michelle Gallero,
Peter Harper, Robert Marasco, Natalie McCrea, Jonathan Polsky, Mary
Jane Rigoroso, Steven Sandonato

SPORTS ILLUSTRATED Director, New Product Development:
Bruce Kaufman

CLASSIC RIVALRIES
Editorial Director: Morin Bishop
    Project Editor: John Bolster
    Managing Editor: Ward Calhoun
    Photography Editor: John S. Blackmar
    Designer: Barbara Chilenskas

CLASSIC RIVALRIES was prepared by
Bishop Books, Inc.
611 Broadway
New York, New York 10012

We welcome your comments and suggestions about Sports Illustrated
Books. Please write to us at:
SPORTS ILLUSTRATED Books
Attention: Book Editors
PO Box 11016
Des Moines, IA 50336-1016

If you would like to order any of our hardcover Collector's Edition books,
please call us at 1-800-327-6388.
(Monday through Friday, 7:00 a.m.- 8:00 p.m. or Saturday,
7:00 a.m.- 6:00 p.m. Central Time).

Contents

Introduction

BY JACK McCALLUM

In sports, as in lovemaking, you're better off with somebody else around. Talk all you want about the romance of shooting hoops alone after midnight, or firing six-irons at a practice green, Hogan-like, until your hands bleed, but the fact remains that it doesn't get real until you test yourself against somebody else. Yo, Phil and Ernie: keep knocking down that pin at dusk, but the time comes when you gotta do it with a Tiger in your twosome. And, so, along comes *Classic Rivalries* to celebrate the essential otherness of sport, the elemental reality that sports are most genuine when you measure yourself against a foil. And, in fencing, against a foil's foil.

Many of us conjure up gentler times when rivalries weren't so intense and sports weren't, as the late Mr. Rogers might've put it, so doggoned mean. Except those times never existed. I don't have the entrant list in front of me, but I'm guessing if say, Thermidides got toasted by Lionones in the 200-yard race at the first recorded Olympic contest in 776 BC, he badly wanted another shot at the L-Dog four years later.

The mythology of our collective boyhood speaks to the magic and wonder of playing catch with our fathers, and, indeed, that is how I learned the game. But baseball never really permeated my consciousness until fourth grade, when Miss Bickel's classroom took on Mr. Boyd's in an epic best-of-three struggle. I can provide details of the Bickelians' glorious victory, but we don't have that much that space.

Rivalries evolve so naturally in sports that we're involved in them almost before we realize it. Few athletic-minded fathers were as uncompetitive as mine, but, as I think back, he instilled a ferocious anti-New York Yankee hatred in me. We didn't just go to World Series games at Yankee Stadium when I was a young kid—we went to *watch the Milwaukee Braves beat the damn Yankees.* (Which they did in 1957 but not in '58.) We didn't go to the old Convention Hall in Philadelphia to watch the Warriors play the Boston Celtics—we went to *watch Wilt Chamberlain dominate Bill Russell.* (Which he usually did but the Warriors somehow always lost.) We didn't brave freezing weather at Franklin Field to watch the 1960 NFL championship game between the Eagles and the Green Bay Packers—we went to *watch Chuck Bednarik stuff Jim Taylor.* Which he did.

Anybody out there remember the great Liberty–Freedom rivalries of the early '70s? Probably not. In my first newspaper job in Bethlehem, Pa., my beat was covering Freedom High sports, then the second cousin to the older and slightly larger Liberty High. Freedom's games—soccer, basketball, baseball and, of course, Friday night football—never meant much to me unless the Patriots were playing Liberty. In my early sportswriting days, my identity seemed somehow interlocked with Freedom's: When they won a big game over Liberty, I was somehow better than the sportswriter who covered Liberty. (I got over that quickly.)

When I began to cover pro and big-time college sports, I found a whole subterranean level of rivalry. Oftentimes, my job was not so much chronicling the rivalries between teams—the obvious ones that the fans think about and the marketing departments trumpet—but the rivalries *within teams.* Interestingly, it wasn't just bad teams, which are bad partly because they squabble and suffer from petty internecine rivalries. Good teams have internal rivalries, too—player vs. coach, player vs. player, even coach vs. coach—and they're the fascinating ones.

Chamberlain (13) frequently towered over Russell (6) in the box score, but Russell's Celtics usually came out ahead on the scoreboard.

The last of the NFL's two-way players, Bednarik (right) made his name decking opponents like Green Bay's Taylor and, famously, New York's Frank Gifford (left).

The first big-time athlete I covered who had a rivalry with his coach was Penn State's Matt Millen, a tough All-America defensive lineman with an impish streak. Millen respected his legendary coach, Joe Paterno, but bristled at some of Paterno's motivational techniques and stratagems, and the two played a fascinating verbal cat-and-mouse game during Millen's four years.

When I began covering the NBA for SPORTS ILLUS-TRATED in the mid-'80s, nobody seemed happier than the runnin' and gunnin' Showtime Los Angeles Lakers, but there was always rivalry between players and coach on that team. Magic Johnson, the smilingest one of them all, was primarily responsible for coach Paul Westhead's firing in 1981 (a little more than one year after Westhead had won the championship) and it wasn't long before Magic and Pat Riley were quiet rivals, even as L.A. went back-to-back in 1987 and '88.

Mind you, that wasn't unusual or even particularly inexplicable. Ego and pride are in voluminous supply in skilled athletes and highly competitive coaches, and there's a constant elbowing for space behind the scenes. "The X's and O's of coaching are overrated," said Chuck Daly, a coach who won championships with the Bad Boy Detroit Pistons in '90 and '91 and a gold medal with the original Dream Team in the '92 Barcelona Games. "It's about keeping control of a team's internal strife, all those little rivalries, being

aware of them but never letting the lid blow off."

Daly knows of what he speaks, for that was a rivalry-prone Pistons team he coached. Even as the Pistons were perhaps heading for an NBA title in the 1988–89 season, the behind-the-scenes rivalry between starting forward Adrian Dantley and team leader Isiah Thomas grew increasingly intense. At midseason, Thomas, in the best NBA tradition of franchise-players-get-what-they-want, legislated a trade to get rid of his rival in favor of his good friend, Mark Aguirre. "We all know it was Isiah who made the trade," said Dantley as he packed his bags for Dallas, a team that would go 38–44 while the Pistons went on to a championship.

But the best rivalries—the ones that fuel both sports and this book—take place between the lines. Sometimes those rivalries are imbalanced, as when the entire Piston team ganged up to stop Michael Jordan in the '80s. In a career so replete with memories and milestones he would have trouble recounting half of them, Jordan remembers with particular fondness the day—May 27, 1991—that his Bulls completed a four-game sweep of Detroit in the Eastern Conference finals, at last putting him on top in this frustrating rivalry with the Pistons.

At the height of that rivalry, it is no exaggeration to say that Jordan and the Pistons despised each other. Sometimes as intriguing, though, are those rivalries with more texture, rivalries with limits. Sticking with the Pistons, Thomas's first two trips to the Finals brought him up against his great friend, Magic (with whom he later had a falling out). As they met at mid-court in the 1988 Finals, they exchanged cheek smooches at the opening tip. Imagine: a rivalry sealed with a kiss—and what drama eventuated when they later squared off and almost exchanged punches.

The best of these type of rivalries is covered, and covered well, in the book. While the basketball world framed the Magic Johnson–Larry Bird rivalry in absolutes—black vs. white, West Coast vs. East Coast, fast break vs. fundamentals, hip-hop Earvin vs. old-school Larry—the combatants themselves had a more nuanced view of their matchups. At its best, theirs was what sports rivalries are supposed to be but rarely are. You respect your opponent. You might even like your opponent. You might even want to hang out with your opponent (as, unbeknownst to almost everyone, Russell hung out with Chamberlain before they went out to destroy each other on the court). But within the time frame of the competition—and that includes between games of

The feisty McEnroe (left) found formidable rivals in both Connors and Borg (right), whose Wimbledon reign he ended.

a long series—you treat your rival like a rival. You don't kiss each other. You don't suck up to each other with excessive compliments. You don't show more camaraderie with your opponent than you do with your teammates.

My own feeling is that, in this particular rivalry, the protagonists got something from each other. Bird, who had the social skills of a crocodile when he entered the league with Magic in '79, learned from Magic that it was okay to give a shout-out to your rival, okay to acknowledge that, yeah, he's a pretty good player. Magic, whose enthusiasm could bubble over into something bogus and unendurable from time

to time, learned from Bird the necessity of limits, of keeping their friendship apart from their rivalry. It's a massive understatement to say that Bird wasn't really a smooching-at-center-court kind of guy.

So *Classic Rivalries* gives us all we want to know about the subtext behind the headline rivalries—the well-chronicled battles of not only Bird and Magic but also of McEnroe and Connors (McEnroe–Borg, too; some guys are feisty enough to be multi-rivaled), Carl Lewis and Ben Johnson and Duke–North Carolina—as well as some of those lost to history. Attention, young readers: the football teams of Harvard and Yale were once powerful enough to command the attention of America; two guys named John Landy and Roger Bannister altered the history of track; and on a long-ago Friday night in the 1960s, the rivalry between two boxers named Emile Griffith and Benny (Kid) Paret was so intense that one of them beat the other to death in the ring.

It's not always sweat and muscle that make up the best rivalries, either. For a couple of years in the '70s, a strange, skinny young egghead named Bobby Fischer, who pushed chess pieces around a board, commanded the attention of the sports world (and, since the Cold War was brewing, also the political world) because of a rivalry with a Russian chess player named Boris Spassky.

Alas, rivalries are almost endless, and book space is not, so there simply wasn't the time to go into every great rivalry that has blossomed since the turn of two centuries. There's no Auburn–Alabama football from the '60s, no Boston College–Boston University hockey from the '70s, and no Michael Johnson–Maurice Greene from the '90s. Worse, there is no Bickel–Boyd from the '50s. But I was around for that one, and I can tell you it was all Bickel.

Beginnings

Now, altogether, loud and clear
Beat Notre Dame
Speak up so the whole world can hear
Beat Notre Dame
From South Bend rooters, take no sass
But boldly bellow out en masse
Those roughnecks Irish shall not pass

—*POPULAR CHEER IN LINCOLN, NEB., NOV, 1925*

TOP 5	ARMY–NAVY
	GRAZIANO–ZALE
	DETROIT–TORONTO
	LOUIS–SCHMELING
	NOTRE DAME–USC

Of course, the good townspeople of Lincoln could not know that their rude words would reshape the sporting landscape. They had no idea how deeply the doggerel reprinted on placards and published in local papers would offend the visitors from Indiana in town for the big football game, prompting the degraded "roughnecks Irish" to call a halt to their series with Nebraska after 11 years. Nor could they have guessed that a representative from USC would be poised to swoop in and, with the aid of his wife, persuade Notre Dame coach Knute Rockne to replace the soon-to-be-vanquished Cornhuskers

Zale (far left) KO'd Graziano in the third round of their rubber match in Newark, NJ, concluding their epic rivalry.

USC received a ticker-tape parade (opposite) after its title-clinching victory over Notre Dame in 1931; seven years earlier, the Irish, led by the Four Horsemen (right, l to r) Don Miller, Elmer Layden, Jim Crowley, and Harry Stuhldreher, galloped to a 10–0 record.

on his schedule with the Trojans. No, it would be wrong to fault the Nebraskans for their coarse welcome: They were merely doing their part to stir up a rivalry.

But the lesson to be learned from their effort is this: A compelling rivalry cannot be induced. Sure, a little vitriol and name-calling can spice things up, but it takes more substantial elements to transform a series of games or matches into highly anticipated, hotly contested showdowns. As they helped to transform sports from recreational diversions into more popular (and bankable) propositions, the best rivalries of the first half of the 20th century contained most, if not all, of these elements: There was frequency (such as Army vs. Navy in college football), familiarity (Maple Leafs vs. Red Wings in pro hockey) or contrasting styles (Tony Zale vs. Rocky Graziano in boxing). Mostly, though, it would take a combination of these ingredients, simmered over time, to cook up a

rivalry. Consider what was required to turn a date between Notre Dame and USC into an annual event known as the Glamour Game.

● SERENDIPITY. In 1925 the Trojans' inability to beat hated Cal drove USC administrators to look longingly at Rockne as a replacement for Elmer (Gloomy Gus) Henderson—despite Henderson's record of 45–2 against other teams. But the Fighting Irish coach was under contract, and so USC graduate manager Gwynn Wilson was charged with attaining the next-best thing: a home-and-home series with Notre Dame. The 26-year-old Wilson and his bride, Marion, attended the Nebraska game, and Rockne invited them to accompany him and discuss the matter on the train ride back to Chicago.

Despite Wilson's entreaties, Rockne declined the offer, saying that the Irish were already spending too much time on the road. "I thought the whole thing was off," Wilson would recall. "But as Rock and I

1908 **Ford introduces the Model T** *1910* **The Boy Scouts of America holds its first meeting**

$65

Purported amount wagered, and won, on Army to beat the heavily-favored Midshipmen in 1913, by a dozen cadets—including injured linebacker and plunge back Dwight Eisenhower. Army won 22–9.

$58.6 million

Amount generated by 20,000 War Bonds sold as part of the "Sixth War Bond Drive," entitling the buyer to a free ticket to the 1944 Army-Navy game. Two weeks before the game, President Franklin D. Roosevelt relocated the contest from Annapolis to Baltimore to provide the extra stadium capacity for fans to see the nation's two top-ranked teams square off.

2

Number of times that Army and Navy have played one another as the No. 1 and No. 2 teams in the Associated Press college football poll. Army won both games, taking the first one 23–7 on Dec. 2, 1944, and winning the second one 32–13 on Dec. 1, 1945.

25

Weekly Associated Press polls from 1936 to 1950 in which Army was the nation's top-ranked team. Army has held the top spot in 27 AP polls, while Navy has never been ranked No. 1.

8

Number of wins and losses, respectively, for the undefeated Cadets and the winless Midshipmen prior to the 1948 game. A 20-point underdog, Navy staged an impressive fourth-quarter comeback to stun Army with a 21–21 tie on Bill Hawkins' fourth-down scoring run.

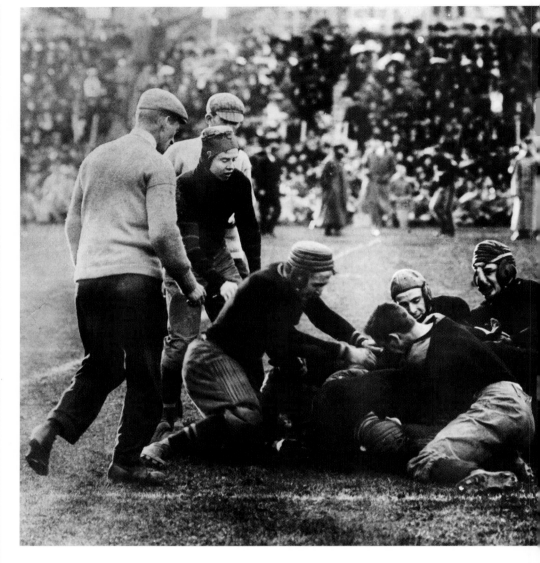

The Midshipmen won the Army–Navy game of 1906 (above), throwing the series' first forward touchdown pass en route to a 10–0 victory.

talked, Marion was with Mrs. Rockne, Bonnie, in her compartment. Marion told Bonnie how nice Southern California was and how hospitable the people were. Well, when Rock went back into the compartment, Bonnie talked him into the game."

● COMPETITIVE BALANCE. On Dec. 7, 1925, a deal was done. Despite his misgivings about extensive travel, Rockne was subjecting his squad to a four-day, 2,300-mile train trek every other year (one way). He would also be facing a team reshaped under new coach Howard Harding Jones, whose no-nonsense

single-wing offense would become so potent that it would earn the Trojans a new nickname: the Thundering Herd. Before Jones arrived at USC, the program had not produced an All-America player in its 36-year history. In 16 seasons under Jones, it produced 19. The improved caliber of the Trojans would be essential in making the Glamour Game.

A burgeoning power that had won the 1924 national championship with a 10–0 record, Notre Dame traveled to L.A. in 1926 for the inaugural game of the series. Their 8–1 record matched USC's, but the single loss was a doozy: The Irish had been stunned 19–0 by Carnegie Tech, a team Rockne took so lightly he had opted to attend the Army-Navy game instead of his own. With six minutes left at the Coliseum, in front of an impassioned crowd of 74,378 fans, Notre Dame trailed 12–7 and appeared to be heading for its second straight loss. But Rockne replaced his star quarterback with little-known southpaw Art Parisien, who rallied the Irish to a 13–12 victory. This would set a pattern: Three of the first four games of the series were decided by one point.

● CONTROVERSY. Before the 7-0-1 Trojans boarded the Golden State Limited on Nov. 22, 1927, they had never traveled east of Arizona for a game, and no West Coast team had ever undertaken so distant a journey. USC was sent off with "the fanfare of trum-

pets and the raucous cheering of several thousand frenzied supporters," the *Los Angeles Times* wrote. "The thunderous ovation will probably be ringing in the gridders' ears when they disembark in Chicago." But on the return trip, the sound that resonated for the Southern Cal players was a third-quarter ruling that negated a safety and preserved a 7–6 Irish victory at Soldier Field, denying the Trojans a shot at the national title. For years, USC fans remembered that loss bitterly, their grievance further inflamed by the makeup of the officiating crew: The umpire, referee and head linesman all hailed from Chicago.

● GRAVITY. In 1928, a 27–14 victory over Notre Dame in the third game of the series propelled USC to a share of the national championship, with Georgia Tech. The following year Rockne, stricken with phlebitis and battling for his life, raised himself out of his wheelchair to deliver a fiery halftime speech with the score tied 6–6. "Go on out there. Go on out there and play 'em off their feet in the first five minutes," he said. "They don't like it. They don't like it. Play 'em. Play 'em. . . . Come on, boys. Rock's watching." Before an estimated 120,000 fans at Soldier Field in Chicago, the unbeaten Irish shot out of the locker room, stormed to the lead and hung on for a 13–12 win. Two weeks later they knocked off Army and wrapped up a national title of their own.

Notre Dame was 9–0 when it traveled west in 1930, yet was considered the underdog against the potent, once-beaten USC team. Thumbing their noses at the oddsmakers, the Irish roared to a 27–0 victory, giving them back-to-back titles and a fitting capstone to Rockne's career; he died four months later in a plane crash, at the age of 43.

Hearly (Hunk) Anderson took over and, in '31, watched his team race to a 14–0 lead in the Glamour Game. But behind the running of Gus Shaver, the passing of Orv Mohler and a last-minute field goal by Johnny Baker, USC erased that deficit in the fourth quarter for a 16–14 victory that clinched the

Sid Abel (left) and the Red Wings battled the Maple Leafs—often literally— seven times in the play- offs during the 1940s.

The assassination of Austria-Hungary's Archduke Ferdinand sparks World War

No. 1 ranking for the season. More than 300,000 fans welcomed the Trojans home from South Bend. When USC seized the national championship again in 1932, it marked the fifth straight year that one of the entrants in the Glamour Game had been so honored. Before 1950, Notre Dame would earn five more titles—and be denied a shot at an unbeaten season by a loss to Southern Cal in 1938.

Such high-stakes, inter-regional competition quickly turned USC–Notre Dame into a football event as seismic as Army–Navy, which had a 36-year head start. The rivalry between the service academies— "the show, the spectacle, the pageant of youth that always is about as thrilling as anything in American sports," the *Washington Post*'s Shirley Povich called it in 1948—was packed with memorable moments. In 1906, the forward pass wobbled into the college football playbook for the first time. During the Midshipmen–Black Knights clash of that year, Navy's Homer Norton completed the series' first touchdown pass, coming up throwing out of punt formation and connecting on a 25-yard score to Jonas Ingram.

The Midshipmen won that landmark game 10–0, but Army would go on to build a slight edge in the first 44 games of the series (22-19-3), leading up to their memorable showdown in 1944. In front of a sellout crowd of 66,639, a significant portion of which

had bought war bonds to get in, Army hoped to nail down its first undefeated season since 1916. Navy had won the previous five meetings between the teams, holding the Cadets to a single touchdown in all of those victories combined, and the Midshipmen were keen to close the alltime series gap even further. The Black Knights clung to a 9–7 lead into the third quarter, then broke the game open behind touchdowns from their All-America backs, Doc (Mr. Inside) Blanchard and Glenn (Mr. Outside) Davis to win 23–7. As Army coach Earl Blaik would say, "It was a case of the country's No. 1 team beating the country's No. 2 team."

That was the case again the following year, when Navy entered the game at 7-0-1 and ranked second, only to lose 32–13 following Blanchard's three-touchdown performance. A third straight win by the Cadets in 1946 helped Army run its three-year record to 27-0-1, but the Cadets were denied a third straight national championship when AP voters chose Notre Dame, which finished 8-0-1. The Midshipmen did not defeat Army again until 1950, when they came to the annual showdown with a 2–6 record and won 14–2, handing the Army juggernaut its only loss that year. The 1950 game stands as one of the biggest upsets of the series.

As the Army–Navy tradition proves, the drumbeat of regular encounters can also drive a rivalry, and

Ben Hogan (rear, with his tie tucked into his shirt) watched his longtime rival Byron Nelson blast out of a sand trap during practice for the 1939 U.S. Open, which Nelson won.

nowhere was this more true than in the early years of the NHL. Formed in 1917, the league never fielded more than 10 teams in its first 25 seasons, and from 1942–43 until expansion began in '67–68, it had only six: Boston, Chicago, Detroit, Montreal, New York and Toronto. That meant not only that players were in a constant battle to hold on to one of the 100 or so steady jobs, but also that they faced each other with grinding regularity, building grudges and exacting revenge. On-ice officials weren't exempt from this vicious cycle; they, too, were roughed up on occasion.

By the 1940s one of the more pugnacious NHL teams was the Toronto Maple Leafs, whose owner, Conn Smythe, was fond of saying, "If you can't beat 'em in the alley, you can't beat 'em on the ice." Another was the Detroit Red Wings, who, hockey writer Trent Frayne said, "carried their sticks like lances and plastered visiting players against the boards as though they were advertisements."

After a 1939–40 Stanley Cup semifinal in which the two teams brawled for 12 minutes, a Toronto executive called the Red Wings "a bunch of hoodlums," prompting Detroit coach Jack Adams to reply, "We're just sorry we can't play the Leafs seven nights in a row." The teams squared off again in the 1942 Stanley Cup finals, where the underdog Red Wings swept the first three games. With his team on the brink of elimination, Toronto's star goalkeeper, Walter (Turk) Broda, seemed to give up the ghost. "Detroit is unbeatable," he said. But Leafs coach Hap Day pulled out all the stops—benching regulars and even tacking a supportive letter from a 14-year-old girl to the locker-room wall—to rally his

club to three straight wins and force a decisive seventh game. Before 16,200 fans at Maple Leaf Gardens, a record crowd in Canada at the time, Toronto left wing Sweeney Schriner scored two goals to lead the Leafs to a 3–1 victory. The unprecedented comeback provided sweet relief after a decade of frustration;

Hogan (left) and Nelson posed at the 1942 Masters, which Nelson won in a dramatic playoff over his boyhood friend.

between 1932–33 and '39–40, the Maple Leafs had lost in the finals six times, including a sweep at the hands of Detroit in 1935–36.

During the rest of the 1940s Detroit and Toronto would meet five times in the postseason. Three shutouts by Toronto goalie Frank McCool, who calmed his ulcers by drinking a quart of milk before each game, helped the Leafs seize a seven-game thriller for the Stanley Cup in 1944–45. Then came a thoroughly impressive three-peat by the Maple Leafs from 1947 to '49, during which they took 12 of 13 games from Detroit, shutting down the Wings' vaunted Production Line of Gordie Howe, Sid Abel and Ted Lindsay. In 1949–50, though, the Red Wings ended that streak with an overtime win in Game 7 of the semifinals, beginning their own run of four championships in six seasons.

Since 1892, when heavyweights John L. Sullivan and Gentleman Jim Corbett engaged in a 21-round slugfest in New Orleans for the heavyweight title, boxing has yielded some of the most ardent all-out feuds—Jack Dempsey against Gene Tunney, Joe Louis versus Billy Conn and Louis against Max Schmeling, to name a few. But the most riveting triptych of fights during the first half of the 20th century were the battles between Thomas Rocco Barbella (Rocky Graziano) and Anthony Florian Zaleski (Tony Zale) from 1946 to '48. Part of the drama came from their contrasting personalities. Graziano, a glib street kid from New York's Lower East Side, was banned by the New York boxing commission for failing to report a bribe and by Illinois as a wartime deserter dishonorably discharged from the Army. Zale was the taciturn product of the steel mills of Gary, Ind., who served a four-year hitch in the Navy and, in 1946, was credited by *Ring Magazine* with "picking boxing up off the floor, where it had been left, in the estimation of the public."

That encomium came after their first title bout, in front of 39,827 fans at Yankee Stadium, which to this day ranks among the best fights of all time. Despite giving away nine years to his opponent, despite being knocked down in the second round, and despite being so groggy that he went to his opponent's corner instead of his own at the end of the fifth, Zale recovered spectacularly to knock out Graziano with a left hook in the sixth. A year later, at Chicago Stadium, the rematch attracted a record gate for an indoor fight of $422,918, with well-known figures from every walk of life—movie stars, politicians, financiers—anticipating another slugfest. Pounded by Graziano's relentless assault and drained by the humidity, Zale succumbed to a TKO in the sixth

"I can't beat the sonofabitch," Johnston (near right) said of his nemesis Tilden, but it was not for lack of trying.

round, surrendering the middleweight crown he had held since 1941. "Mama, the bad boy done it," shouted Graziano above the din. But Rocky's brawling style did not fare so well in the '48 rubber match, which, like the other fights, ended in a knockout—once again delivered by the 35-year-old Zale's punishing left hook.

Rivalries in most other sports did not occasion as much bloodshed, but they were fierce in their own ways. Two of the best golfers in the pro tour's history, Ben Hogan and Byron Nelson, grew up caddying at Glen Garden Country Club in Fort Worth. Though head-to-head duels between the Texans were infrequent, they did meet in the first 18-hole playoff in Masters history, in 1942, when each was in his prime. During an 11-hole stretch in that playoff, Nelson gained five strokes on Hogan—even though Hogan had played those holes at one under par—to rally to victory.

Big Bill Tilden (at 6' 2") and Little Bill Johnston (5' 8½") battled with and against one another in tennis throughout the 1920s, though there could be no debate about their relative standing. When teaming up for the U.S. Davis Cup team they were invincible, dominating international matches from 1920 to '26, an unmatched run of success. But when placed on opposite sides of the net, Big Bill almost invariably had the upper hand. Starting in 1919, they faced each other in the U.S. finals six times in seven years. Johnston's lone victory during that stretch, in the first meeting, would turn out to be his undoing—it prompted Big Bill to remake his backhand, thereby rounding out his game to devastating effect. Johnston came close to winning the following year, bowing in a five-set match that at the time was deemed the finest ever. After Tilden won the '25 U.S. title at Forest Hills, Johnston said, "I can't beat him; I can't beat the sonofabitch; I can't beat him."

Tilden dedicated his memoirs to Little Bill, who died of tuberculosis in 1946 at the age of 51. Johnston was, after all, his rival.

Perennial contenders in the early days of the NFL, the Bears and the Giants met in the league's first two official championship games, in 1933 and '34, splitting them and setting the tone for a rivalry that would endure for decades. Chicago quarterback Sid Luckman (above) threw for a record seven touchdowns in a November 1943 rout of New York at the Polo Grounds.

Bruising Chicago running back Bronko Nagurski carried two tacklers with him during the 1934 NFL championship, famously known as the Sneaker Game. In 9° weather, Nagurski's Bears rumbled over the frozen Polo Grounds turf to a 13–3 lead, but when the Giants traded their cleats for basketball shoes at half-time, they used their newfound traction to ring up 27 points in the fourth quarter and win, 30–13.

Where Eagles Dare: Bill Tilden and Bill Johnston perched at the pinnacle of American men's tennis to the exclusion of almost every other player from 1919 to 1925. They met in six U.S. Open finals during that span, with three of those matches going five sets, including the epic finale of their rivalry, at the 1925 U.S. Open final in Forest Hills, which went to Tilden (foreground) 4–6, 11–9, 6–3, 4–6, 6–3.

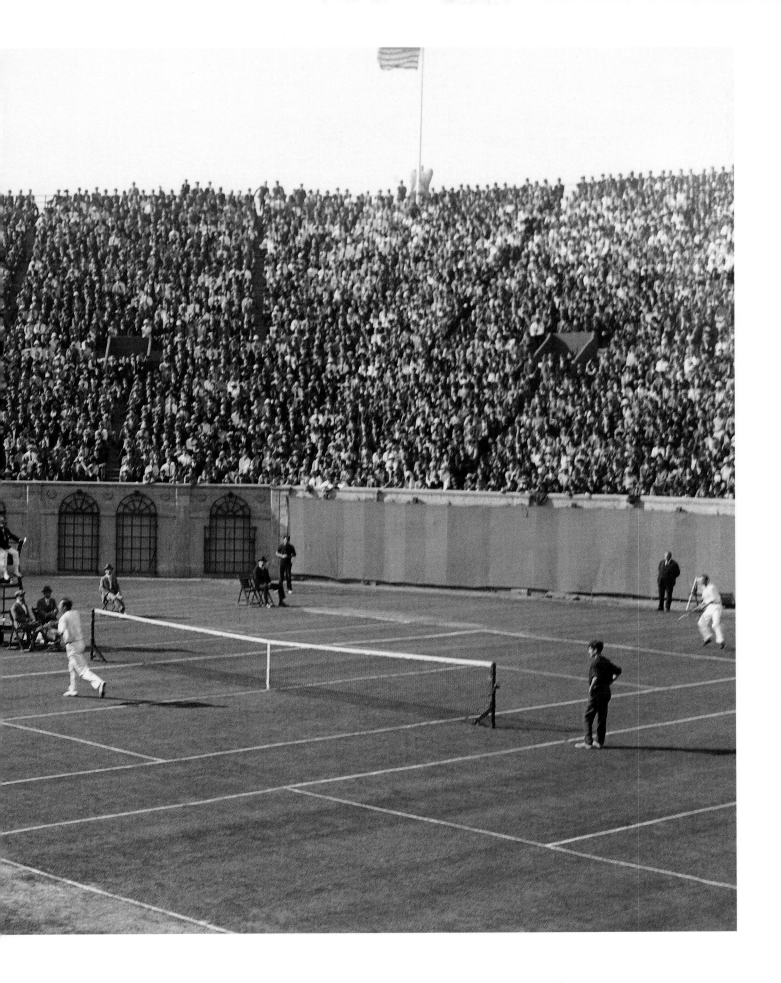

Referred to in some circles as simply *The Game*, the Harvard–Yale football rivalry began in 1875 and is the nation's third longest-running series, with 118 meetings through 2002. Yale won the 1916 game (above) 6–3, prompting students to shoot off "Roman candles and fireworks, writhe in snake dances and carouse far into the night," according to the New York Times.

A Yale defender tackled a Harvard running back after a 35-yard gain in the second quarter of their 1940 meeting, which Harvard won 28–0. The Game may not have the mainstream appeal it did when the teams were national contenders in the first half of the 20th century, but the 2002 edition drew a sellout crowd of 30,323.

Ushering in one of the NFL's primal rivalries during its infancy was legendary receiver Don Hutson of the Green Bay Packers, the league's player of the year in 1941 and '42.

Hutson's Packers clashed repeatedly with the Chicago Bears of Sid Luckman and Bronko Nagurski, sowing the seeds of a rivalry that endures today.

Dominating his era with grace and power, Bill Tilden held the No. 1 ranking for a record six consecutive years. He won three Wimbledon titles to go with his seven U.S. championships.

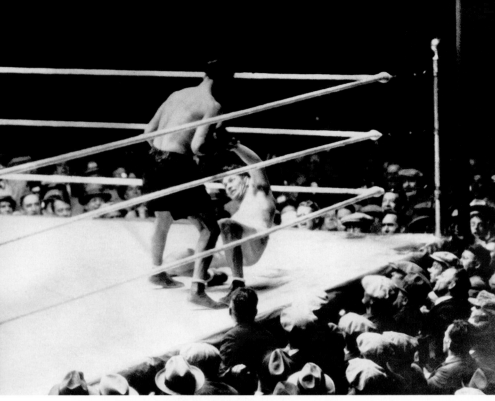

One of boxing's most controversial rivalries involved Jack
Dempsey and Gene Tunney,
whose rematch in 1927
became known as the "long
count" fight. After decking
Tunney in the seventh round
(above), Dempsey forgot to
obey a new rule dictating that
he walk to a neutral corner,
thereby delaying the referee's
count and allowing Tunney to
recover and win a decision.

In September 1892, former
bareknuckle boxers John L.
Sullivan (above, left) and
Gentleman Jim Corbett
fought the first heavyweight

title bout in which the contes-
tants used gloves. Corbett,
who is credited with inventing
the jab, won the epic clash
by KO in the 21st round.

Legendary heavyweight champion Joe Louis (above, left) found one of his greatest rivals in former light heavyweight champ Billy Conn, who was winning their 1941 title fight after 12 rounds before falling to a Louis knockout punch in the 13th. Louis won the 1946 rematch as well.

Tinged with nationalistic, racial, and political overtones, the rivalry between Joe Louis of the U.S. and Germany's Max Schmeling struck deep chords. Fans in Yorkville (above), a German neighborhood of New York City, celebrated Schmeling's victory in a non-title fight in 1936 (top). Schmeling won by knockout in the 12th round of the bout, handing Louis his first loss as a professional.

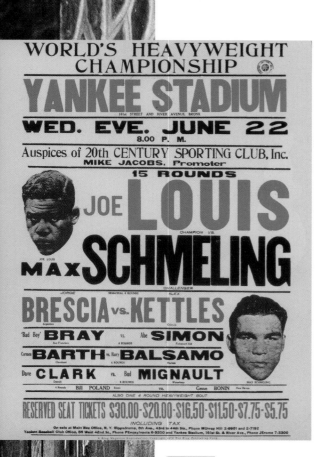

WORLD'S HEAVYWEIGHT CHAMPIONSHIP

YANKEE STADIUM
161st STREET AND RIVER AVENUE, BRONX

WED. EVE. JUNE 22
8.00 P. M.

Auspices of 20th CENTURY SPORTING CLUB, Inc.
MIKE JACOBS, Promoter

15 ROUNDS

JOE **LOUIS**
CHAMPION VS.
JOE LOUIS

MAX **SCHMELING**
CHALLENGER

JORGE   SEMI-FINAL 6 ROUNDS   ALEX
BRESCIA VS. **KETTLES**
Argentina   Chile

'Bad Boy' **BRAY**   vs.   Abe **SIMON**
San Francisco   6 ROUNDS   Paterson, N.J.

Carmen **BARTH** vs. Harry **BALSAMO**
Cleveland   6 ROUNDS   Harlem

Dave **CLARK** vs. Bud **MIGNAULT**
Detroit   6 ROUNDS   Waterbury

4 Rounds   Bill **POLAND** Bronx   vs.   Gene **BONIN** New Haven

ALSO ONE 4 ROUND HEAVYWEIGHT BOUT

RESERVED SEAT TICKETS $30.00 · $20.00 · $16.50 · $11.50 · $7.75 · $5.75
INCLUDING TAX

On sale at Main Box Office, N. Y. Hippodrome, 8th Ave., 43rd to 44th Sts., Phone MUrray Hill 2-6601 and 2-7192
Yankee Baseball Club Office, 55 West 42nd St., Phone PEnnsylvania 6-9300 and Yankee Stadium, 161st St. & River Ave., Phone JErome 7-3300

Beneath a portrait of the champion, Harlem residents gathered in a local bar to listen to the radio broadcast of the second Joe Louis–Max Schmeling bout, which, as the poster (above) touted, was scheduled for 15 rounds at Yankee Stadium. Much to the delight of fans in Harlem and most of the U.S., 14 of those rounds would be unnecessary as Louis knocked out Schmeling in the first round, retaining his undisputed heavyweight title and avenging the only loss of his career to date.

1950s

The 1950s forever will be known as a decade of expansion in sports, but for all of the new territories the burgeoning professional leagues colonized, and for all of the transcontinental matchups they established as a result, the greatest rivalry of the decade was a three-headed affair perpetuated by a trio of long-standing teams from the same city: New York. Big Apple fans had a sumptuous baseball buffet at their disposal during the 1950s. They could take the East Side IRT to the Bronx to watch the Yankees, then as now the dominant team in the game. Across the Harlem River from Yankee Stadium, at the Polo Grounds in Upper Manhattan, New Yorkers could watch the Giants and their feisty manager, Leo Durocher. Finally, they could take the subway out to Ebbets Field in Brooklyn, where, of

The Dodgers' Jackie Robinson stole home against Yankees catcher Yogi Berra during Game 1 of the 1955 World Series.

course, they'd find the Dodgers, lovable underdogs and perfect foils for the city's other two teams. Affectionately nicknamed "Dem Bums," the Dodgers' perennial motto was "Wait Till Next Year."

Pledging one's allegiance to one of these teams meant two things: rooting intently for that team, of course, and hating the other two with an equal, fiery passion. The rivalry between the Dodgers and Giants was fiercest, as they met 22 times every year during the regular season. "It was like pulling teeth whenever they got to play," said actress Laraine Day, Durocher's wife. "When Leo left home for each game against the Dodgers, he could have been a man taking off for the Crusades." The feeling in Brooklyn was mutual, as the Dodgers cringed at anything that reminded them of the Giants and their black-and-orange-trimmed uniforms. "We Dodgers even disliked Halloween because its colors were orange and black," said Brooklyn outfielder Duke Snider.

When the two National League teams, the Dodgers and Giants, were done fighting it out with each other, more often than not the one left standing would get a crack at the Yanks. Either the Dodgers or Giants won the NL every year from 1951 to '56, and the Yankees, it seemed, won the American League every year. (It only seemed that way: They actually won the AL every year of the decade except 1954 and '59.) Their dominance was so expected—and infuriating—that a musical celebrating their hoped-for demise opened on Broadway in the early days of the 1955 season. Titled *Damn Yankees*, the play starred Gwen Verdon and Ray Walston and ran for 1,019 performances.

The New York baseball rivalries hit a peak in 1951, when the ill will that had been simmering for years produced the most compelling pennant race the sport has ever seen, climaxing in baseball's most memorable moment: Bobby Thomson's Miracle of Coogan's Bluff homer off Ralph Branca on October 3.

The bad blood between Durocher and the Brooklyn players had its roots in the late '40s, when, oddly enough, Durocher was managing the Dodgers. In 1947, Brooklyn general manager Branch Rickey made history by promoting second baseman Jackie Robinson to the majors, giving major league baseball its first black player and shattering the game's long-standing color barrier. Some of the more benighted Dodgers were against the idea, but Durocher, at Rickey's behest, supported the move and fought the naysayers head-on. Even though he was suspended (for consorting with gamblers) for Robinson's rookie season, Durocher paved the way for the second baseman's historic entry into the game. Robinson quickly became one of the best players in the league despite immeasurable pressure from the national spotlight, hostile peers and often vicious fans.

But after helping the Dodgers reach the 1947 World Series, where they lost in seven games to—you guessed it—the Yankees, Robinson showed up to spring training in '48 overweight and out of shape. Durocher, back at the helm, was livid. "What in the world happened to you?" he asked Robinson in front of a crowd of reporters. "You look like an old woman. Look at all that fat around your midsection. . . . Why, you can't even bend over!" With the press looking on, Durocher worked, and needled, Robinson mercilessly in the heat of Ciudad Trujillo, the Dominican Republic site of the Dodgers training camp.

That tension set the tone for the season, in which the Dodgers dropped off from their NL-winning form of '47; they would finish 84–70, seven and a half games out of first place. But Brooklyn could take solace in the fact that the Giants were struggling as well. New York president Horace Stoneham wanted to fire his manager, Mel Ott, in early July of '48. He was interested in Burt Shotton, who had managed the Dodgers during

Yankees fans taunted the Brooklyn faithful with the perennial Dodgers slogan of the 1950s, "Wait Till Next Year." New York beat Brooklyn in the Fall Classic in 1947, '49, '52 and '53; in '55, 'next year' finally arrived, as the Dodgers won a seven-game thriller.

third full year with the team, with a win and 11 straight losses, much to the delight of the Dodgers—especially Robinson, who never forgot the grief he took from Durocher. "Leo, I can smell Laraine's perfume!" Robinson would yell into the New York dugout as he danced along the basepaths. Durocher, a stylish dresser known for an unstinting use of cologne, usually responded with unprintable phrases.

Brooklyn had been under new management since the previous season, as Walter O'Malley, a conflicted man if there ever was one, took over as president of the team. O'Malley had been born in the Bronx—Yankee territory—and grew up a Giants fan. Now he was running the Dodgers. His first move was to choose Charlie Dressen, a firebrand in the Durocher mold, to be his new manager. Beanballs became almost routine as the Dodgers–Giants rivalry heated up, and Dressen gave his pitchers clear instructions. "I told my pitchers to get two of them for every one of our guys they knock down," he said. The team responded to his aggressive style and came blazing out of the gate. By late May, Brooklyn had opened up a 12-game lead over the Giants in the NL standings.

With his team languishing in the middle of the pack, Durocher decided to bring up a young centerfielder named Willie Mays from Minneapolis, where Mays was playing for the Millers.

"You don't want me, Mr. Durocher," Mays told Leo when he got the call.

"Now just why is it that I don't want you, son?" Mays said that he couldn't hit big-league pitching.

"What are you hitting now?" said Durocher.

".477."

"Do you think you could hit two-f------fifty for me?"

Durocher's suspension. Rickey said no, but then made a shocking offer: Stoneham could have Durocher. So on July 16, Leo the Lip, Public Enemy No. 1 among Giants fans, became the Giants' manager. (Shotton took over the Dodgers.) It was just as confusing for Brooklyn fans, who had loved Durocher for years but now had to view him as a mortal enemy.

Durocher dismantled the Giants and built what he liked to call "my kind of team"—the implication being that there had been something wrong with the team prior to his arrival, and that he was just the man to fix it. But the Giants failed to improve significantly under Durocher. They began the 1951 season, Durocher's

Fellow rookies and soon-to-be baseball icons Mickey Mantle of the Yankees (left) and Willie Mays of the Giants posed prior to the 1951 World Series.

And with that, a great sub-rivalry was born, at least in the minds of New York's rabid baseball fans: Which of the three future Hall of Fame centerfielders in New York—Mays, Yankees rookie Mickey Mantle, or Dodgers fourth-year man Duke Snider—was the best? The parties involved didn't show much interest in it, but the question received enough attention in the taverns and schoolyards and offices of the five boroughs to more than make up for the players' disinterest.

Mays would establish his greatness by season's end,

Giant Heist: New York outfielder Monte Irvin made a dramatic steal of home plate during Game 1 of the 1951 World Series against the Yankees.

winning the rookie-of-the-year award, but he started slowly, struggling to adjust to big-league pitching, and the Giants continued to lag behind the pace in the NL. On August 11, they were 13½ games behind Brooklyn, and the season seemed a lost cause. But the next day, New York took two from Philadelphia and began a tremendous late-season surge. They won 16 in a row to close out the month, and took 37 of their final 44 games to catch the Dodgers with two games left in the regular season.

"I don't know if they put us in a state of shock," said

Monroe graces the first cover of Playboy   1954   *Alan Freed coins the term "rock 'n' roll"*

Brooklyn outfielder Andy Pafko. "But we did start to get anxious as it came down to the end. I guess we were lucky to wind up in a tie." Indeed, the Dodgers salvaged that tie with a 14th-inning homer (by Robinson) against Philadelphia in their final game of the season, leaving them level with the Giants atop the NL at 96–58, and forcing a best-of-three playoff to decide the pennant.

As dramatic as the Giants' late-season charge had been, it would be topped for excitement by the three-

While Robinson (foreground) and Branca stood glumly in the infield, the Giants thronged home plate to greet Thomson following his historic clout.

game playoff. The teams split the first two games, and were tied 1–1 in the eighth inning of the deciding game at the Polo Grounds. Brooklyn scored three runs in the top of the eighth, thanks in part to some sloppy fielding by Bobby Thomson at third base. Thomson had also killed a Giants rally in the first inning when he was thrown out trying to stretch a single into a double.

The Staten Island Scot, as Thomson was nicknamed, would get a glorious chance to redeem himself in the

1954 **Brown v. Board of Education strikes down segregation** *1955* *Jonas Salk's polio*

bottom of the ninth. While many of their fans began trickling toward the exits, convinced that New York's astounding late-season surge would go for naught after all, the Giants hit two singles and a double to make the score 4–2. New York had men on second and third with one out and Thomson coming to bat when Dressen opted to pull starter Don Newcombe in favor of 25-year-old fastballer Branca—a decision that Brooklyn fans argue about to this day. Branca had started and lost the opening game of the series just two days earlier, surrendering a home run to none other than Thomson in the 3–1 defeat.

Thomson took a fastball for strike one, then drove the next pitch, another heater, toward the short porch in left field. Pafko could only watch as the ball sailed over his head and landed in the seats 320 feet from home plate. After a second of stunned silence, the crowd burst into delirium. In the WMCA radio booth, Giants play-by-play man Russ Hodges immortalized the moment in apoplectic triplicate: "The Giants win the pennant, the Giants win the pennant, the Giants win the pennant! I don't believe it, I don't believe it, I do NOT believe it!" While the Dodgers hung their heads, the Giants bounded around joyously, and confetti flew from the stands. Catcher Eddie Stanky leaped onto Durocher's back and the two of them trotted down the third baseline after Thomson, headed toward the happy mob of his teammates at home plate.

BY THE NUMBERS

13
Number of games by which the Dodgers led the Giants in the National League standings on August, 12, 1951. New York won 37 of its final 44 games to tie Brooklyn at the end of the year and force a three-game playoff.

4
Runs scored by the Giants in the bottom of the ninth inning of the third game of the 1951 NL playoff series. Whitey Luckman's one out double drove in Alvin Dark with the second Giants run of the game, setting up Bobby Thomson's walk-off three-run homer—the Shot Heard Round The World—off of Brooklyn's Ralph Branca.

7
Number of home runs Thomson had hit that season against Brooklyn prior to his pennant winning blast. Thomson hit 32 home runs during the 1951 regular season.

7
NL pennants captured by either the Giants or Dodgers during the 1950s. The Dodgers won five and finished in second place another three times, including twice to the Giants. During the decade, the Dodgers had a 117–106 head-to-head advantage over the Giants.

8–0
Score of the first major-league game ever played on the West Coast, a Giants home win over the Dodgers on April 15, 1958, at Seals Stadium in San Francisco.

At a Red Cross center in Brooklyn, people donating blood were so enraged by the presence of a Giants fan among them that they screamed for the nurse to drain him dry.

Alas, it was the Giants who were drained, emotionally at least, after winning their first pennant since 1937 in such dramatic fashion. They didn't have enough left to match the Yankees in the World Series and went down to defeat in six games. The Bombers would beat Brooklyn in '52 and '53 for good measure, provoking cries of "Wait Till Next Year" from Bushwick to Bensonhurst.

The Giants would bounce back to win the World Series in '54—against Cleveland, though, not the Yanks—and in 1955, "next year" would finally arrive in Brooklyn. Yes, the Bums bested the Bombers in the 1955 Fall Classic, as Johnny Podres shut down the Yanks 2–0 in Game 7 for his second win of the Series. It was the first time that the Yankees lost a World Series to a team other than the Cardinals, who beat them in 1926 and '42. Of course, the Yankees took their revenge the following year, beating Brooklyn in seven games, the fifth a 2–0 win powered by pitcher Don Larsen's perfect game—a feat unmatched in the 98-year history of the Fall Classic.

While New York enjoyed a Golden Age of baseball rivalries in the 1950s, Cleveland experienced a football bonanza during that decade. In 1945, a group of businessmen founded the All-America Football Conference,

vaccine is approved for widespread use   James Dean is killed in an auto accident

placing one of their franchises in Cleveland, which already had an NFL team, the Rams. But that team's owner, Daniel Reeves, gave up on the city after only 32,178 fans showed up to see the team win the 1945 NFL championship. (In the fans' defense, it was 2° that day.) Instead of battling the newcomers for the Cleveland market, Reeves moved his team to Los Angeles. There was little love lost. Years later, Jim Benton, an end on the '45 Rams team, said, "I was glad to move out of there. I never was crazy about Cleveland, to be honest with you. The weather was the No. 1 reason. And No. 2, I just felt we would have better support than in Cleveland."

Cleveland's new team, the Browns, dominated the fledgling AAFC, winning the league in each of the four years it existed. Prior to the 1950 season, the NFL

Cleveland's Dante Lavelli (80) never received this pass, but the Browns snared the 1954 NFL title, routing Detroit 56–10.

absorbed the AAFC's Cleveland, Baltimore and San Francisco franchises. The newcomers, particularly the Browns, were not exactly welcomed with open arms. A few years before the merger, NFL commissioner Bert Bell had called the AAFC a "Humpty Dumpty league," and the established NFL teams were eager to see the Browns put in their place, to prove that Cleveland's four AAFC titles were meaningless. For their first NFL game, the Browns traveled to Philadelphia to play the defending NFL champion Eagles. They trounced Philadelphia 35–10, then waltzed through the regular season with a 10–2 record.

That set up a title game showdown with their erstwhile neighbors, the Rams, who returned to Cleveland with a chip on their collective shoulder. Trailing 28–27, with 1:50 left, the Browns took over at their own 32-yard line. Quarterback Otto Graham methodically drove his team down the field, setting up a 16-yard Lou Groza field goal with 28 seconds remaining. Groza booted it cleanly through the uprights, and not even Bell could deny that the old AAFC powerhouse was legitimate. That evening he called Cleveland "the greatest team ever to play football." The Rams redeemed themselves the following year in another thrilling NFL title game, downing Cleveland 24–17 on a 73-yard touchdown pass from Norm Van Brocklin to Tom Fears.

By reaching the championship game in each of their

first two seasons in the NFL, the Browns had proved beyond a shadow of a doubt that they belonged in the established league, but they didn't stop there. The Browns reached *six* consecutive NFL title games to start the decade, winning three of them. And if it wasn't the Rams waiting for them in the championship game during that span, it was another fierce rival with ties to the Rust Belt, the Detroit Lions. Detroit's hard-living,

Rugged fullback Marion Motley (76) and the Browns edged the Rams 30–28 in the 1950 NFL championship game.

loosey-goosey quarterback, Bobby Layne, was the Dionysian foil for the strait-laced Northwestern grad Graham, who ran Cleveland coach Paul Brown's offense with machine-like efficiency.

The Lions and the Browns met for the NFL championship in '52, '53 and '54, with the Lions winning close games the first two years before Cleveland blew them out 56–10 in '54. Graham threw for three touchdowns and ran for

is published *The Soviet Union launches* Sputnik *and sparks a "space race" with the U.S.*

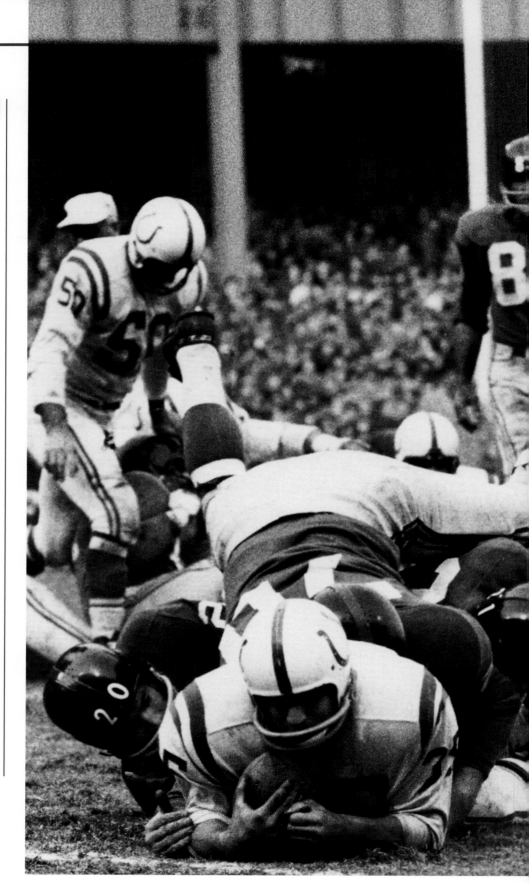

BY THE NUMBERS

40 million

Estimated number of viewers who tuned into the NBC broadcast of the 1958 NFL title game on Dec. 28, 1958, between the Baltimore Colts and the New York Giants. Commonly considered the best game in NFL history, it ended with a one-yard touchdown plunge by Baltimore's Alan Ameche.

$100,000

Amount paid by NBC to the home team, the Giants, for the rights to broadcast the game live from Yankee Stadium. Paying only the home team for TV rights was the accepted practice in those days.

$500

Amount paid to Ameche to appear in the audience of *The Ed Sullivan Show* on the evening after he scored pro football's most famous touchdown.

$750

Amount turned down by Colts quarterback Johnny Unitas to appear in the Ed Sullivan audience.

12

Number of players who participated in the game who would eventually be enshrined in the Pro Football Hall of Fame in Canton, Ohio. Three coaches involved in the game have also been inducted.

24

Fourth-quarter points scored by the Colts to erase a 9–7 deficit and break open the rematch of the '58 classic, the 1959 NFL title game. Final score: Baltimore 31, New York 16.

Elvis Presley's Ed Sullivan appearance draws 82.6% of the national television audience

three more in that game. The following year he led Cleveland back to the title game for a rubber match against the Rams. Graham ran for two scores and threw for two, leading Cleveland to a 38–14 win. The future Hall of Famer announced his retirement after the game, much to the relief of the Detroit and Los Angeles faithful.

While the Rust Belt's football rivalries were just heating up, the region's hockey grudges had been simmering for years. The NHL had consisted of only six teams since 1942, an arrangement that served to reinforce the maxim, "familiarity breeds contempt." Teams often shared trains during home-and-home series, but the rides were far from cordial. "I never spoke to any of them," said Detroit Red Wings forward Ted Lindsay. "I hated them, and they hated me. It was the way it was and the way it should be. It was wonderful."

The Wings of that era were especially unfriendly with the Montreal Canadiens. Detroit was the defending champion at the start of the 1950–51 season and stormed through the schedule with a record 101 points—only to be bounced from the playoffs by the Habs in the first round. The teams shared one striking similarity—each was led by a remarkably talented, tough, high-scoring right wing. Detroit had Gordie Howe; Montreal had the Rocket, Maurice Richard. They were the NHL's answer to Mays and Mantle, two stars who played the same position and inspired fierce debate among fans over who was better. Both were willing to mix it up, but they had a grudging respect for each other. During the 1951–52 season, Montreal held a night in Richard's honor. As the Rocket was skating off the ice, Howe stopped him. The crowd, seeing Howe take off his glove, took a second to make sure that there wasn't going to be a fight. When they saw

Baltimore's Alan Ameche fell under a swarm of tacklers during the 1958 NFL title game against the Giants, a nationally televised sudden-death overtime thriller that dramatically boosted pro football's national appeal. The Colts won 23–17.

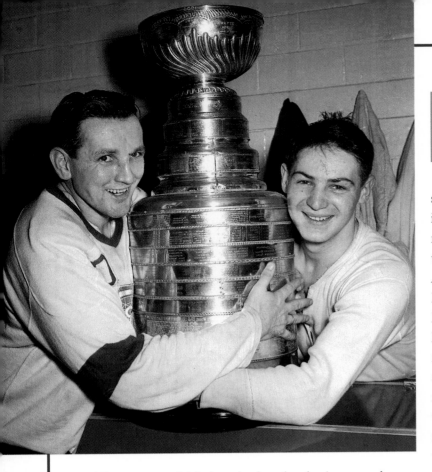

Howe extend his hand, they broke into applause. Richard took it graciously, then watched as Howe went out and scored a pivotal goal for the Wings.

The teams met in the 1952 Finals, and Detroit swept the Canadiens. Though his team was clearly outplayed, Montreal coach Dick Irvin refused the traditional post-series handshake, instead stalking off to the locker room and slamming the door in the face of the Detroit writers. The scene replayed itself in 1954, when the Wings won in seven games, the last one decided in overtime. Again, Irvin refused to shake hands. "I wouldn't have meant it," said Irvin. "I refuse to be a hypocrite." Detroit again won a seven-game thriller for the Cup over the Canadiens in 1955, thanks largely to the fact that Richard was suspended for punching a linesman late in the season, a punishment that sparked a riot in Montreal. Irvin's team would finally beat the Wings in the Finals in 1956.

Not all of the rivalries of the era were bitter, though. Runners John Landy and Roger Bannister spent much of 1953 and '54 trying to break the fabled four-minute barrier for the mile. Bannister finally, and famously, did so at Iffley Road track in Oxford on May 6, 1954, clocking 3:59.4. Forty-six days later, Landy followed Bannister across the four-minute threshold, shaving more than a second off Bannister's world record. On August 7, 1954, the two milers finally went head-to-head, at the British Empire Games in Vancouver. Landy held the lead as they approached the tape, but when he looked back over his left shoulder to see where Bannister was, the lanky Brit blew by him on the right side and won in 3:58.8. For the second time in three months, Landy had been upstaged by Bannister. But he took his defeat nobly. A few days after the race, a stunning revelation hit the papers: Landy had cut his foot two days before the race when he stepped on a photographer's flashbulb. The cut required four stitches, but Landy had sworn his doctor—and a reporter who happened to find out—to secrecy. After the race, he steadfastly denied he had even received stitches, because he didn't want to taint his rival's victory. Landy proved that classic rivalries have their chivalric side as well.

Some three years after the Mile of the Century, the face of major league baseball underwent a massive transformation. Following the 1957 season, the Dodgers vacated Ebbets Field for the (figuratively and literally) greener pastures of Los Angeles. Robinson had been traded to the Giants before the season, but decided to retire instead. To the very end, though, he saved a little something for his bitterest rivals—in 1956 he hit .275 and stole only 12 bases, but at the Polo Grounds that season, he hit .394 and swiped seven bags. The Giants followed in the Dodgers' footsteps, relocating to San Francisco during the same offseason. The moves paid financial dividends for both teams, but provided a bitter end of an era for their fans, leaving them bereft of three classic rivalries.
—Mark Bechtel

1959 *Fidel Castro assumes total control in Cuba   Berry Gordy founds Motown Record*

Giants fans geared up for Game 2 of the 1951 playoff to decide the National League pennant. Their team would lose that day, but come back to win Game 3 with baseball's most famous home run.

England's Roger Bannister (329) outkicked John Landy of Australia (300), the world record holder at the time, to win the Mile of the Century at the Empire Games in Vancouver on Aug. 7, 1954.

Both men broke the four-minute barrier in the fabled race, a first in track and field history. His place in the sport's pantheon secure, Bannister would retire at the end of the season.

The Canadiens and their Hall of Fame goalie, Jacques Plante (above right) dominated the NHL in the 1950s, but they did not lack for worthy rivals, including the Toronto Maple Leafs and Bob Pulford (left). Montreal won the 1959 Stanley Cup over the Leafs, claiming a record fourth consecutive NHL title.

In 1953, Maureen Connolly (right, receiving the Wightman Cup) became the first woman to achieve the Grand Slam; she defeated her toughest rival, Doris Hart (left), in three of the four major finals.

Maurice (Rocket) Richard of the Canadiens slipped the puck past Boston goalie Red Henry. In addition to several fierce playoff clashes and their contentious regular-season tilts, the Bruins and Montreal met in the Stanley Cup finals three times during the 1950s, with the Canadiens winning all three series.

Nebraska running back Bobby Reynolds (12) raced 13 yards for a touchdown during the Cornhuskers' 49–35 loss to Oklahoma in 1950. Though the rivalry was intense, Nebraska could do little in the 1950s against the Oklahoma juggernaut, which reeled off an NCAA–record 47 consecutive wins from 1953 to '57.

Cleveland quarterback Otto Graham prepared to throw downfield during the 1954 NFL championship game against the Lions. Graham had a career day, throwing for three touchdowns and running for three more as the Browns won 56–10, avenging their losses to Detroit in the previous two NFL title games.

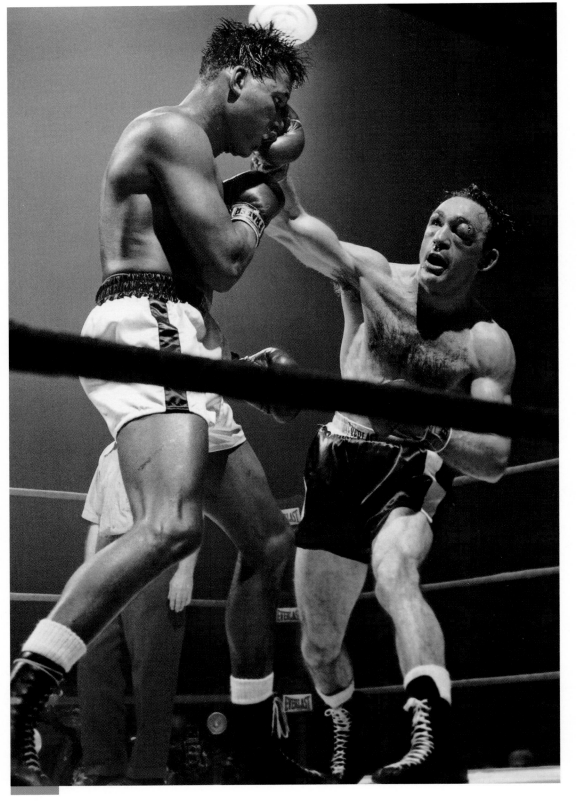

He may have been nick-named Crazy Legs, but the Rams' Elroy Hirsch (40) showed graceful form as he gathered in a six-yard completion in front of Cleveland's Cliff Lewis during the 1951 NFL title game. It was the third straight trip to the championship game for the Rams, and it proved to be the charm, as they finally won a title, downing Cleveland 24–17 and avenging their 30–28 loss to the Browns in the previous season's finale. The teams met for the title again in '55 and Cleveland won in a rout, 38–14.

No rivlaries are more ferocious than those in boxing, as Carmen Basilio (above right) would attest. He met Sugar Ray Robinson (left) for the middleweight title in 1957 and '58. Basilio took the first clash and lost the second, both on decisions after 15 brutal rounds. Each bout was named Fight of the Year by Ring magazine.

1960s

TOP 5

CHAMBERLAIN–RUSSELL
NICKLAUS–PALMER
LISTON–CLAY/ALI
NFL–AFL
JOHNSON–YANG

The outcome would be decided within five minutes—or, to be more precise, in the final split seconds of the last of those minutes. As the new decade dawned, the coveted title of the world's greatest all-around athlete was at stake, and one of two men—friends, teammates and the most devoted of rivals—would seize it.

For two years they had trained side by side, eyeing each other with a mixture of appreciation and concern, aspiring to the same singular and epic achievement. So when they started the 1,500-meter run, the final event of the tautest, tensest decathlon in Olympic history, Rafer Johnson of the United States and Taiwan's C.K. Yang each knew that the price of his own glory would be the other's heartache. "I'm used to pressure," Johnson

Teammates and training partners at UCLA, Johnson (near right) and Yang dueled for the 1960 Olympic decathlon gold medal.

would say later. "I've been under it every time he and I walk out on the track together."

The 1960s will be remembered for a range of conflicts, from Nixon versus Humphrey to John versus Paul to Ginger versus Mary Ann, and the head-to-head matchups in sports were among the most fascinating. Did you root for the irresistible force (Wilt Chamberlain) or the immovable object (Bill Russell)? The glowering former convict (Sonny Liston) or the garrulous Muslim convert (Muhammad Ali)? The fastidious up-and-comer (Jack Nicklaus) or the roll-the-dice free swinger (Arnold Palmer)? The choices were starkly antipodean: Which one you liked often said a lot about who you were and where you stood on a variety of issues.

In the matter of Johnson vs. Yang, though, preference was mostly a matter of geography. They both attended UCLA, but Johnson grew up in Texas and California, played basketball and served as student body president. Yang Chuan-Kang was born on the island of Formosa (currently known as Taiwan), where he showed sufficient promise to earn his government's permission to train in the U.S. Even though he spoke no English, Yang enrolled at UCLA in 1959, while Johnson was recovering from a car accident in which he suffered a severe muscular strain in his lower spine. "I was lucky Yang was here when I started to work out again," Johnson said. "He's a real hard-nosed competitor. Boy, he doesn't even run a warmup lap without trying to win. He's like me: He doesn't like to be second."

In July 1960, in Eugene, Ore., a fully recovered Johnson amassed 8,683 points to smash the decathlon world record held by Vasily Kuznetsov of the Soviet Union; Yang finished second at that meet, and broke the Russian's mark as well. Less than two months later, the collegiate teammates and their coach, Ducky Drake, debarked for what Johnson, the silver medalist in the decathlon at the Melbourne Olympics in 1956, had decided would be the final competition of his career: the Summer Games in Rome.

Despite losing four of five events to Yang, Johnson held a slim first-day edge. Back and forth they went the following day, capturing the hearts and imaginations of the Italian spectators. Yang upset Johnson in the 110-meter high hurdles. Johnson won the discus. Yang finished higher in the pole vault. Johnson picked up points in the javelin. After nine events, the American held a 68-point lead over his college teammate and Taiwanese national. For the first time in Olympic history, the decathlon title would come down to the event most dreaded by the decathletes, the 1,500-meter run. To become the first gold medalist in his nation's history, Yang would have to beat Johnson in the race, a "metric mile," by 10 seconds. It was a tall order, indeed, but it was possible—Yang's personal best was 4:36.0; Johnson's was 4:54.2.

More than 12 hours after the day's competition had begun, they readied themselves for the race of their lives. Coaching both men, Drake told Johnson to dog Yang throughout and be prepared for a "hellish sprint"; he advised Yang to build up as big an advantage as possible then try to grind Johnson down on the final lap. His battered gray straw hat on his knee, a clammy hand running over his bald head, Drake watched Yang assume a lead and try to shake Johnson, who clung to his heels entering the final lap. With the roar in the stands building, Yang stretched his edge to one meter; his rival made up that ground in five long strides. Again Yang surged ahead by a meter, but Johnson's pipestem legs churned furiously until the finish line came into view, and completely spent, his momentum carried him across.

He finished in 4:49.7, only 1.2 seconds behind Yang, a result that left Yang with 8,334 points and Johnson with 8,392 and the gold medal. They wobbled for a few yards, then fell against each other to stay upright as the

Johnson (near left) broke the tape a step ahead of Yang in the 400-meter run at the 1958 U.S. decathlon championship in Palmyra, N.J. Johnson, who won the event, would be named Sports Illustrated's *Sportsman of the Year for 1958.*

Monroe stars in her last film, The Misfits   *The Cuban missile crisis threatens world peace*

crowd thundered its approval all around them. "You'll never see another decathlon like this," Drake said. "There ought to be some way to have a tie." Yang had won seven of 10 events, but his prize was not gold. "I knew he would win," Yang said of Johnson. "He is that way. I have trained with him. I heard him there behind me and I knew he would win."

That same air of inevitability accompanied the 7' 1", 275-pound Wilt (the Big Dipper) Chamberlain when he joined the NBA's Philadelphia Warriors out of Kansas before the 1959–60 season. Many observers assumed that he would be the league's dominant force in the middle. Among them was Bill Russell, who had led the Boston Celtics to the championship with his defense and rebounding the previous season. "After I played Wilt the first time," Russell recalled, "I said, 'Let's see. He's four or five inches taller. He's 40 or 50 pounds heavier. His vertical leap is as good as mine. He can get up and down the floor as well as I can. And he's smart. The real problem with all this is that I have to show up!' "

Russell, of course, would prove more than up to the challenge. "People say it was the greatest individual rivalry they've ever seen," he said. "I agree with that." During a 10-year span, the two giants played one another 142 times in the regular season and in the playoffs. Russell averaged 14.5 points and 23.7 rebounds in those games, while Chamberlain averaged an astounding 28.7 points and 28.7 boards per game for the Warriors, 76ers and Lakers against Russell. But basketball is a team game, and despite Chamberlain's herculean efforts, Russell's Celtics won 85 of those meetings compared to the 57 that Chamberlain's teams won, and Boston won nine titles with Russell at center. Chamberlain won one NBA title in the 1960s, following the 1966–67 season. (He would add another in '71–72.). Often, even the Dipper's most spectacular performances went for naught. As a rookie he pulled down 55

The titanic rivalry between Russell (near right) and Chamberlain has been called the greatest individual matchup in sports history. Russell, the cornerstone of Boston's 1960s NBA dynasty, agrees with that assessment.

rebounds against Boston—an NBA record that still stands—and his team lost 132–129. Two seasons later he racked up 62 points against Russell—and his team lost again, 145–136.

There was little sympathy for the Dipper who, as the bigger man, was seldom seen as the underdog. "Nobody loves Goliath," as Alex Hannum, Chamberlain's coach in Philadelphia, put it. Nor, in dispensing its favor, did the public tend to factor in Russell's more potent supporting casts, which included seven future Hall of Famers. "Somewhere along the way Russell became the intellectual, the sensitive man, the more human, the more humane," said Chamberlain's teammate and friend Tom Meschery. "And Wilt wasn't supposed to be any of those things. Well, that was a bad rap. Wilt was every bit as good a person as Bill, and you could tell how much he was hurt by the way he was perceived."

Indeed, as much as their immense physical talents, the players' psychic interplay made the rivalry riveting. Was Wilt as driven to win as Russ? Did the fans' dim view of Chamberlain affect his game in any way? Did Russell heap praise on his foe to soften him up? Were they indeed close? Chamberlain insisted that though they battled bitterly on the court, they were friendly off it. He recounted settling down to a game of cards on a plane ride they shared in 1965, after a 76ers win over the Celts. Before they started, Russell said he had something to show Chamberlain, and after fishing through his wallet, produced a license to carry a gun. "You win this game," Russell said, "and I'm going to shoot you dead."

During the same year that Johnson outdueled Yang and Russell first bested Chamberlain in the playoffs, the American pro football landscape underwent a transformation as the American Football League, the brainchild of Texas businessman Lamar Hunt, made its debut. The fourth upstart league to use the AFL tag since 1926, this version of the circuit would prove, after the usual

1963 *JFK is assassinated   Martin Luther King Jr. addresses 250,000 in Washington*

growing pains, to be far and away the most successful. It also created an instant rivalry with the established National Football League. Teams from the rival leagues would not meet on the field until 1967, but they began competing fiercely right away—for star players, for television revenues, for fans and most importantly, to the AFL at least, for respect.

That last commodity would prove hard to come by. Members of the NFL camp referred to the AFL as a "Mickey Mouse League." Despite winning the AFL's

Defending Masters champ Nicklaus (rear) helped 1964 titlist Palmer into the winner's green jacket. Their roles would be reversed the following year.

Western Division in their first season, the Los Angeles Chargers relocated to San Diego the following year because they could not outdraw the NFL's Rams, who went 4-7-1 that year. Respect aside, the new league quickly sent the message that it meant business, landing 1959 Heisman Trophy winner Billy Cannon of Louisiana State even though the NFL's Rams had already signed him to a contract. A judge ruled that the NFL's contract, which had been offered before Cannon's final game as a collegian, was invalid.

1964 **The Beatles arrive in New York   The Civil Rights Act becomes law** *1965* **The miniskir**

The war was on, and the two leagues went to great lengths, to say the least, to protect their prospective draft picks from the rival circuit. The NFL went so far as to create a group called Operation Hand Holding, which consisted of escorts whose job it was to shield potential signees from the clutches of the AFL. Oakland Raiders owner Al Davis created a "war chest" for the sole purpose of luring NFL quarterbacks to the AFL. In 1965, the AFL scored its greatest coup with the New York Jets' signing of quarterback Joe Namath of Alabama, which placed a bona fide star in the nation's media capital. Two years later Namath would become the first pro quarterback to throw for 4,000 yards in a season.

Still, the AFL was regarded as an ugly duckling. Before the 1966 season, the rival circuits announced a truce, agreeing to meet in a championship game after that season, to share a common draft in '67 and to merge into a single league in 1970. Before the first AFL–NFL meeting, later dubbed Super Bowl I, Kansas City coach Hank Stram said, "We are playing this game for every team, every player, every coach and every official in the AFL." After the NFL's Green Bay won the game 35–10, Packers coach Vince Lombardi said, "All right. Kansas City doesn't compare with the top teams in the NFL. That's what you wanted me to say—and now I've said it."

The Packers would win Super Bowl II as well, but the upstart AFL would win the next two, with victory in

BY THE NUMBERS

17
Record for most consecutive years on the PGA Tour with at least one victory, shared by Jack Nicklaus (1962–78) and Arnold Palmer (1955–71).

7
Number of strokes that Palmer trailed 20-year old amateur Nicklaus during the final round of the 1960 U.S. Open at Cherry Hills before staging the greatest comeback in the history of the event. Palmer shot a 65 and beat the young Nicklaus by two strokes.

40.6
Percent of major tournaments won by either Nicklaus or Palmer from 1960 to '67. Nicklaus won seven ('63, '65, '66 Masters; '62, '67 U.S. Open; '66 British Open; '63 PGA Championship) and Palmer won six ('60, '62, '64 Masters; '60 U.S. Open; '61, '62 British Open) of the 32 majors played during that span.

$1,990,823
Combined prize money won by Nicklaus ($996,521) and Palmer ($994,302) during the 1960s. Between the two of them they topped the money list six times during the decade and placed second another six times.

$82
Amount that separated first-place Nicklaus ($113,285) from second-place Palmer ($113,203) on the final money list for the 1964 season.

Super Bowl III coming after Namath had brashly and famously guaranteed it. Final score: Jets 16, Colts 7. The new breed had established its credentials.

Golf experienced a similar out-with-the-old, in-with-the-new process in the early '60s, as a 20-year-old upstart from Ohio State edged into preeminence. Jack Nicklaus didn't win the 1960 U.S. Open at Cherry Hills in Denver, but his second-place finish was the highest by an amateur in 27 years. Capturing the national title with one of his trademark charges was Arnold Palmer, who began the final day seven strokes off the pace, birdied six of his first seven holes and fired a 65, a record for the tournament's final round.

At 30, Palmer was the driving force behind the PGA Tour's rising popularity, a brash battler to whom no lie was unplayable and no putt daunting. Others had pitched their cigarettes and hitched their trousers before taking a shot but none had done it with such excitement-heightening purposefulness. Palmer's swashbuckling style and frequent brinksmanship fit perfectly in the burgeoning medium of television. As the number of TV sets in the U.S. swelled and the live coverage of events increased, so did the ranks of his fans—known as Arnie's Army.

Nicklaus could hardly have been more different. Chubby, with a flat-top haircut, he had little of Palmer's charismatic appeal. Though his swing was powerful and graceful, his shots were the product of laborious calculation,

and he often played a round without uttering a word. "On the course he is a study in utter concentration," wrote *Time* magazine, "cold, phlegmatic, withdrawn."

The contrast was never clearer than at the 1962 Open at Oakmont, where they squared off in an 18-hole play-off. In his first season as a pro, Nicklaus was attempting to become the youngest U.S. champ in 39 years; Palmer already held five major professional titles and was playing roughly 30 miles from his hometown of Latrobe, Pa. Nicklaus didn't flinch at the full force of Arnie's Army; in fact, he took advantage of it to play aggressively and seize a four-stroke lead through eight holes. "A big gallery around the green is the biggest advantage a player can have," he said. "If you miss the green, you know the ball isn't going very far." He shot 71 to Arnie's 74 on Sunday. As a friend of Nicklaus's later observed, "The first time he went into the forest, he shot Robin Hood."

At the Masters two years later, Robin Hood shot back, holding off Nicklaus to become the event's first four-time winner. But that would be Palmer's last major, as Nicklaus dominated the rest of the decade, ringing up seven major championships. (He would go on to win a record 18 professional majors in his career.) In 1965 he entered the third round at Augusta tied with Palmer and Gary Player, then went out in 31 en route to a record total of 274. "Palmer and Nicklaus played superbly," legendary champion Bobby Jones said. "Nicklaus plays a game with which I am not familiar."

The decade's fiercest rivalry in boxing belonged to welterweights Emile Griffith and Benny (Kid) Paret, who fought three times within a 12-month stretch in 1961 and '62. Griffith, a native of the Virgin Islands who lived in Queens, N.Y., took Paret's title in the first bout with a 13th-round knockout; Kid, who emigrated from Cuba to Miami, reclaimed his championship in a controversial split decision. The tension built at the weigh-in before the Madison Square Garden rub-ber match, when, for the second time, Paret called Griffith maricón—a Spanish slur for homosexual.

The 24-year-old Griffith took the first five rounds on all cards, but a left hook by Paret in the sixth staggered him along the ropes. In the 10th Griffith's head cleared and he stung Kid with a right, then pummeled him some 30 times without opposition. Two rounds later, with Paret sagging against the middle turnbuckle, Griffith unleashed 15 right uppercuts and several left hooks before the fight was stopped. "As Paret went down," ringside observer Norman Mailer wrote, "the sound of Griffith's punches echoed in the mind like a heavy axe in the distance chopping into a wet log."

Paret slippped into a coma. He was taken to a hospital, where he died nine days later from hemorrhages in his brain. He was 25. An editorial in the Vatican daily, *L'Osservatore Romano*, decried the essence of the sport, "Who can foresee the final result when each contender defends himself to the ruin of the other?"

Two years after that tragic episode, the light heavyweight gold medalist from the Rome Olympics, who had moved up a weight class, challenged Charles (Sonny) Liston, a 31-year-old acclaimed by some as the best heavyweight since Joe Louis—or even since Jack Dempsey. One of 25 siblings from rural Arkansas, Liston moved to St. Louis in his teens and was soon serving concurrent five-year terms for armed robbery. He learned to box in prison, and when he was paroled his career took off—until he landed back in jail for assaulting a St. Louis policeman. Out again, he seized Floyd Patterson's title in 1962 with a first-round knockout, then KO'd Patterson again in the first round to retain it.

While Liston was 215 pounds of pure monosyllabic menace, Cassius Clay moved his feet, hands and mouth—often simultaneously—with rapid-fire splendor. "Float like a butterfly, sting like a bee," he repeated in the days leading up to his showdown with Liston in

Ringside attendants rushed to Paret's aid after Griffith's barrage at Madison Square Garden. Sadly, they were unable to help him.

BY THE NUMBERS

$360,000
Difference in the amounts earned by Sonny Liston and Muhammad Ali for their two heavyweight title fights. The former champ Liston made $1,200,657 while the new champ Ali took home $840,657.

93
Percent of sportswriters in attendance in Miami Beach who, when polled before the first Liston–Clay fight on Feb. 25, 1964, said Sonny Liston would win.

2,434
Spectators at St. Dominic's Rectory in Lewiston, Maine for the Ali–Liston rematch on May 25, 1965, the smallest crowd ever to see a heavyweight title fight.

102
Number of seconds of boxing action those spectators witnessed as Ali knocked out Liston at the 1 minute, 42 second mark of the first round.

14
Number of consecutive victories for Sonny Liston after losing the second Ali bout. Though he did not get another title shot, Liston fought 16 times from June 1966 to June 1970, winning 15 (14 by knockout) and losing one. He died in December 1970.

1968 The U.S.S.R. invades Czechoslovakia   Martin Luther King, Jr. and Robert Kennedy

Miami, for which he was a 7–1 underdog. At the weigh-in, the Louisville Lip put on a long, hysterical show designed to upset Liston, and it proved devastatingly effective. Sonny had murderous thoughts on his mind when he rushed from his corner at the opening bell, and as his usually lethal left hook missed its mark, Clay took to the attack and goaded him further. "Come on," he shouted before splitting Liston's left cheekbone with a sharp right. "Come on, you bum."

Though Clay nearly quit the fight before the fifth round because a caustic applied to Liston's cut had gotten into his eyes and nearly blinded him, his work was finished in the sixth, when Liston tore a tendon in his left biceps. They met again nine months later in Lewiston, Me., by which time Clay had converted to Islam and changed his name to Muhammad Ali. Midway through the first round he knocked out Liston with his "anchor punch." Some observers claimed that Liston took a dive, calling the anchor punch a "phantom punch," but subsequent scrutiny of the fight film has left little doubt about the potency of the right Ali delivered.

Ali's outspokenness on civil rights and Vietnam irked some and emboldened others; in a decade of deep divisions among races and generations, he often served as a lightning rod. He was stripped of his title in 1967 for refusing to be inducted into the armed services, a development that generated a torrent of opinions both for and against his stance. But there had always been unanimity concerning his boxing bona fides: No one doubted that he was a deserving champion. "It's going to be terrible on the ears," wrote columnist Jim Murray after the Lewiston bout in '65, "but Cassius is right back where you have to listen to him and he's coming in loud and clear." —H.H.

are killed   1969   *Woodstock draws 500,000 fans   Neil Armstrong walks on the moon*

The rivalry between the AFL and the NFL peaked in Super Bowl III, when Joe Namath (above) guaranteed—and delivered—victory for his 17-point underdog Jets against the NFL's Baltimore Colts.

While Namath (12) tasted sweet victory against Baltimore in Super Bowl III, he often ate mud when buried under a pile of AFL rival Oakland Raiders, including the 6' 8", 275-pound Ben Davidson (83). The Jets and Raiders staged several memorable clashes in the 1960s, including the infamous "Heidi Game" of '68, and the tense AFL championship of that year, won 27–23 by the Jets.

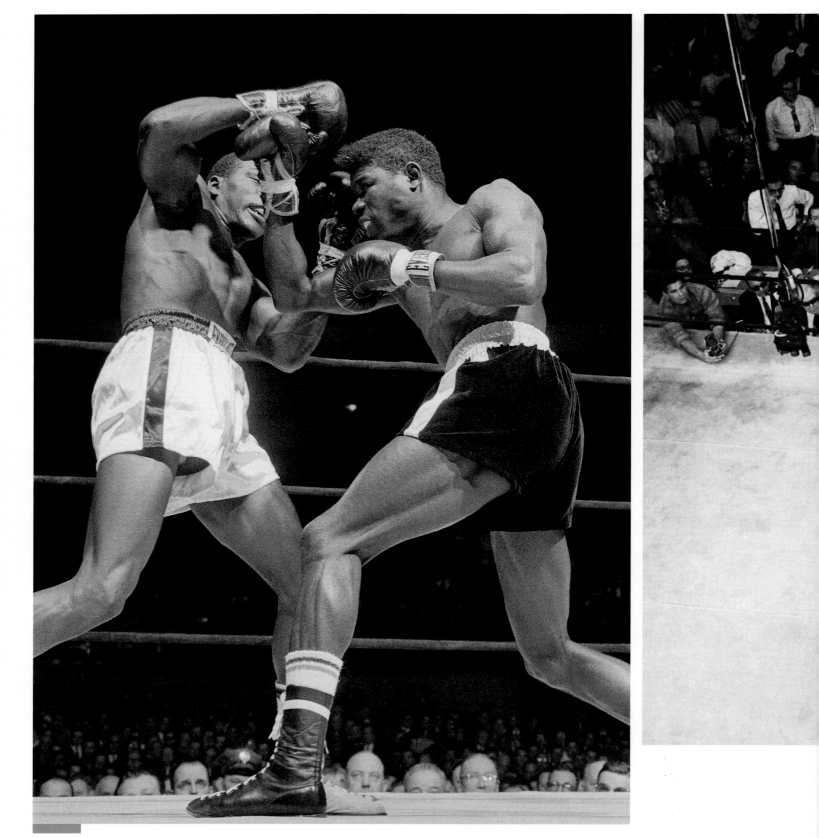

The rivalry between welter-weights Benny (Kid) Paret (white trunks) and Emile Griffith turned deadly in their third bout, at Madison Square Garden in March 1962. Griffith trapped Paret in a corner in the 12th round and hit him nearly 20 times before the referee intervened. The barrage left Paret in a coma, and he died nine days later.

Proving that his unexpected victory the previous year was no fluke, Muhammad Ali (arms raised) dropped Sonny Liston in the first round of their heavyweight title rematch in Lewiston, Me., in May 1965. Many fans missed the knockout blow, prompting suspicion, but subsequent scrutiny of the fight film has established that the so-called "Phantom Punch" was indeed real. Considered the most fearsome heavyweight of his time, Liston never fought for the title again.

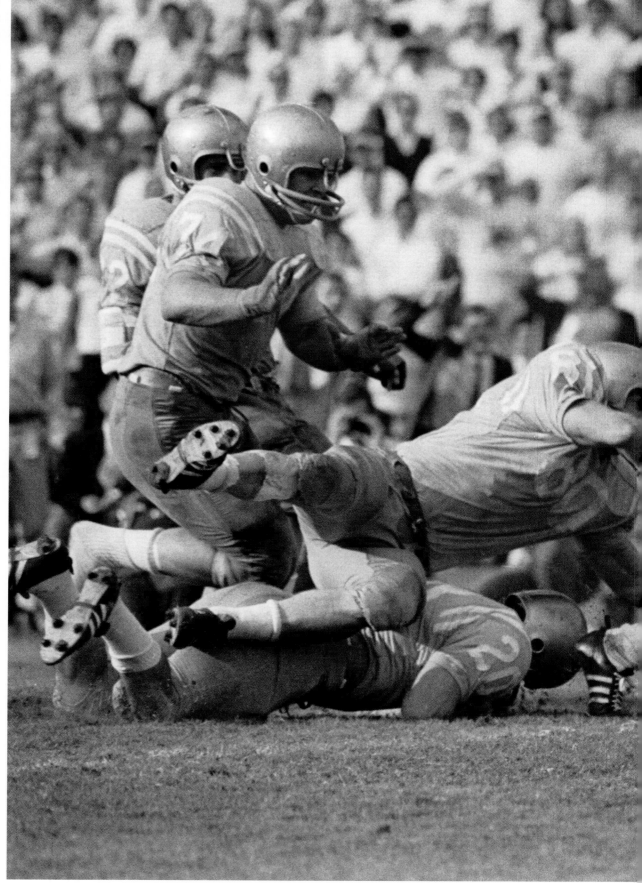

Southern Cal running back O.J. Simpson dashed up the middle for his second touchdown of the game during the Trojans' 21–20 victory over archrivals UCLA in 1967. Southern Cal would go on to win the Rose Bowl and the national title that year. The USC–UCLA rivalry enjoyed a golden age in the '60s, when one or both teams landed in the Top 10 seven times.

Green Bay quarterback Bart Starr turned to make a handoff against Oakland during Super Bowl II at the Orange Bowl in Miami. The NFL champion Packers came into the game as heavy favorites over the AFL's Raiders, and they did not disappoint, pulling away in the third quarter to win 33–14. Starr was named MVP of the game, and the Packers' victory gave the NFL a 2–0 advantage over the AFL in championship meetings, but the younger circuit would establish its credibility in Super Bowl III the following year.

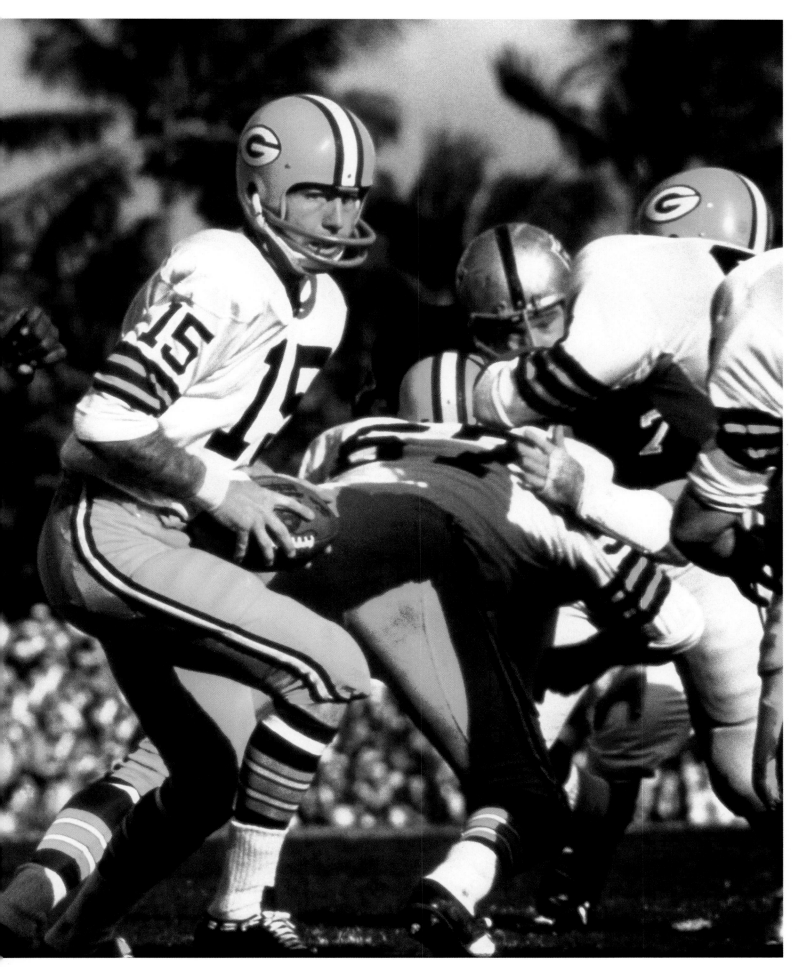

Green Bay's Herb Adderly (26, partially obscured) pounced on Dallas quarterback Don Meredith's fumble during the third quarter of the 1967 NFL title game. Known as the Ice Bowl, this classic took place in sub-zero temperatures and reprised the thriller the teams played in the previous year's title tilt. Green Bay came out on top in both games, winning the Ice Bowl 21–17 on a dramatic quarterback sneak by Bart Starr with 16 seconds remaining.

Richard Petty (far right) and David Pearson (17) found themselves in a familiar position at Darlington in 1967: neck-and-neck. Petty went on to win the race, as well as the NASCAR season points title (with a record 27 victories). The two rivals would take turns winning NASCAR championships during the 1960s, with Petty winning in '64 and '67, and Pearson triumphing in '66, '68 and '69.

In an image emblematic of arguably the greatest individual rivalry in sports history, the 76ers' Wilt Chamberlain skied for a rebound against the Celtics' Bill Russell (6) in 1965. Chamberlain often won the individual battle of numbers in their meetings, but Russell's Celtics usually prevailed on the scoreboard. They won nine NBA titles in the 1960s, including six in a row to start the decade.

The 1962 Masters champion, Arnold Palmer (rear), fits the fabled green jacket over the shoulders of his successor and budding rival, Jack Nicklaus, who won the 1963 tournament by one stroke over Tony Lema. It was the first of Nicklaus's record six victories at Augusta. Palmer would reclaim the green jacket the following year, defeating Nicklaus and Dave Marr by six strokes.

Oakland fullback Pete Banaszak (40) followed the formidable frames of Gene Upshaw (63) and Wayne Hawkins (65) around left end during a 1967 game against AFL Western Division rivals the Chiefs. The rivalry was preserved, with no loss of intensity, when the teams were absorbed into the NFL.

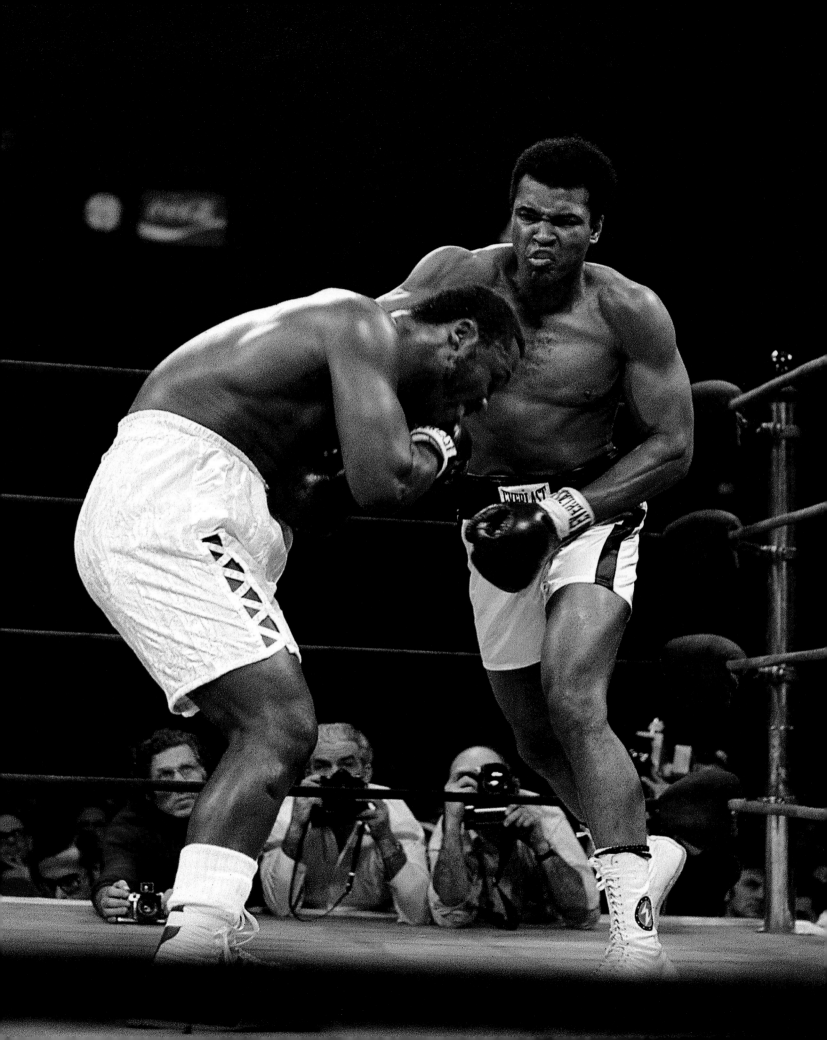

1970s

TOP 5
ALI–FRAZIER
ALYDAR–AFFIRMED
STEELERS–RAIDERS
YANKEES–ROYALS
COWBOYS–STEELERS

At the dawn of the 1970s, America was a nation divided. The primary source of the fragmentation was the war in Vietnam—a war into which Muhammad Ali, the heavyweight champion of the world, had refused to be drafted three years earlier. He was arrested for his stance, lost his belt and was banned from the ring. Ali's stand, made on religious grounds, transformed the heavyweight into a hero in some circles, a villain in others. The brash boxer from Louisville had become the most famous anti-war protester in the country.

While Ali languished in exile, undefeated Philadelphia brawler Joe Frazier won the heavyweight title, and defended it several times before Ali was reinstated—thanks in part to the efforts of Frazier, who lobbied on his behalf—

Ali (near left) took a decision from Frazier in New York City in the second installment of their epic trilogy.

83

1970s

in 1970. The two fighters became fast friends, and during a car ride from Philadelphia to New York, Ali told Frazier how big a windfall a bout between the two of them would be. Even bigger, he said, if they appeared to despise one another. A little subplot, Ali reasoned, would go a long way. Frazier didn't appreciate the notion quite as keenly as Ali. When they arrived in New York, Frazier got out of the car to buy some shoes and, while a crowd gathered, Ali lit into his future rival. "He's got my title! I want my title! He ain't the champ, he's the chump."

Frazier understood that Ali was only fanning the flames of hype, whetting public appetite for a matchup of two undefeated heavyweights. After Ali won two warmup bouts by TKO, he was granted a shot at Frazier's title. Frazier figured the taunting would stop, but Ali's words kept coming, and with more vitriol. "Joe Frazier is too ugly to be champ," Ali said. Frazier's attempted ripostes only backfired. "Joe Frazier is too dumb to be champ," Ali said. "The heavyweight champ should be smart and pretty, like me. Ask Joe Frazier, 'How do you feel, champ?' He'll say, 'Duh, duh, duh.'"

These displays infuriated Frazier, and they also touched a nerve with Americans who resented Ali for refusing the draft. Ali was unperturbed. In fact, the responses only added fuel to his fire. Since a large majority of the people who found Ali obnoxious and wanted to see him shut up once and for all were white, Ali painted Frazier as a pawn of the establishment, the white man's champ. Ali wouldn't let anyone forget that Frazier had visited Richard Nixon at the White House (Frazier deemed it rude to turn down an invitation) or that he was friendly with Philadelphia police commissioner (and later mayor) Frank Rizzo, who had once arrested peaceful demonstrators after they assembled to convince Philadelphia's schools to teach more black history. (Frazier liked Rizzo because the mayor had provided him and his family 24-hour protection when he received death threats before the fight). "Joe Frazier is an Uncle Tom," Ali said. "Ninety-eight percent of my people are for me. They identify with my struggle. Anybody black who thinks Frazier can whup me is an Uncle Tom."

Not that Frazier had come from a well-to-do background. "I grew up like the black man—he didn't," said Frazier. "I cooked the liquor. I cut the wood. I worked the farm. I lived in the ghetto." Alas, Frazier was nowhere near as adept as his opponent at manipulating public opinion, and Ali entered the ring at Madison Square Garden on March 8, 1971, with the support of a wide swath of the public, who saw him as a hero for standing up to what they considered an unjust war. Frazier, for his part, entered the ring pissed off.

It was the most eagerly anticipated fight in boxing history. The fighters got a then-whopping $2.5 million

1971 **All in the Family** *encapsulates the nation's divisions*   *The microprocessor is born*

each. Twenty thousand people packed the Garden, 300 million more watched it on television. Frank Sinatra shot the fight for *Life* magazine, Cliff Robertson did commentary for the television feed. As a study in social commentary it was fascinating: Ali, the loudmouth militant Muslim, supported by liberals, doves and beatniks, and Frazier, the son of a sharecropper, suddenly a hero of the upper classes.

As a fight, it outstripped its most outlandish hype.

Each man landed big blows, but neither would acknowledge having received one. The fighters constantly mocked each other, shaking their heads as if to ask the other if that was the best he could do. The louder the crowd chanted for Ali, the more Frazier dug in demonstrating a resolve that eventually won some of the crowd over to his side. By the time the 15th round arrived, they

> *Ali found himself in an unaccustomed position—on the seat of his pants—during the 15th round of his brutal first meeting with Frazier.*

had no idea who they were screaming for. They just knew to scream, because they were witnessing the greatest fight they had ever seen. Twenty-six seconds into the round, Frazier threw a left hook. Launching it, he looked like he was reaching into his back pocket to take his wallet out. Yet the punch was quick, and Ali couldn't duck it. It caught him flush on the right side of his face, and the former champ went down, an experience to which he, and his fans, were quite unaccustomed. (Years later, Frazier would evoke David and Goliath to describe that epic evening, with one difference: "David had a slingshot. I had a left hook.") Ali somehow got back to his feet and finished the fight, but Frazier won a unanimous decision. Both men required hospitalization after the bout, and when Frazier missed the postfight press conference rumors swirled that he had died.

The inevitable rematch was markedly different. Frazier had lost the belt to George Foreman. Time had sapped the ferocity from the anti-war debate, eliminating many of the socio-political issues that contributed to the first fight's atmosphere. The '70s—the bell-bottom decade—were in full swing. But there was still plenty of animosity between Ali and Frazier. Just days before the fight, they tussled in a TV studio after Ali called Frazier ignorant. Ali won a 12-round decision, but it felt like a letdown compared to the first fight.

After Ali reestablished his greatness, vanquishing George Foreman in Zaire for the heavyweight championship, a rubber match with Frazier for the belt was set. Ali was paid $4.5 million and Frazier $2 million for the fight, which was held in the Philippines on October 1, 1975. The locale provided Ali some great material for his pre-Rap spiels: "It will be a killa and a chilla and a thrilla when I get the gorilla in Manila," he sang. It was all theater, of course, but some observers thought that Ali carried it a bit too far.

Frazier fumed, and after losing the early rounds, came storming back in the middle portion of the fight. The bout crescendoed with exchanges that equaled any of the flurries from their first encounter in Madison Square Garden for unbridled fury. Eschewing his artful, graceful style, Ali stood toe-to-toe with Frazier for 14 rounds, and gradually wore him down. Frazier didn't answer the bell for the 15th. Again, both men were badly battered, and Ali, who was 33, sensed that things would never be the same again. "We went to Manila as champions, me

Cold War Fallout: Bobby Fischer of the U.S. (below right) pondered a move during a politically charged chess match with world champion Boris Spassky of the Soviet Union in 1970; two years later, the U.S. Olympic basketball team had its celebration cut short by a dubious official decision that enabled the U.S.S.R. to score the winning bucket in the gold-medal game (bottom).

and Joe, and we came back as old men," he said.

Ali was right. Neither was ever the same fighter, but their rivalry had concluded with a genuine battle for the ages, and it stands among the greatest matchups in sports history. After the Thrilla Ali tried to apologize to Frazier through his 15-year-old son, Marvis. "He should come to me, son," said Frazier. "He should say it to my face." Ali issued another apology in March 2001.

The 1970s featured other rivalries enacted against the backdrop of the era's politics. In 1972, the world chess champion, Boris Spassky of Russia, was scheduled to meet the top challenger, an eccentric American named Bobby Fischer, in Reykjavik, Iceland. But Fischer wavered about playing, largely because he wanted more money. At the height of the Cold War, the U.S. government wasn't about to watch Fischer back down. No less an official than Secretary of State Henry Kissinger got him on the phone. "In short," Kissinger said, "I told Fischer to get his butt over to Iceland." Fischer eventually agreed to play when his pay was upped to $250,000.

With the financial arrangements taken care of, Fischer began complaining about other matters. He was afraid, he said, that the Russians would shoot his plane down. He arrived safely, of course, and when the tournament started he griped about intrusive television cameras and the proximity of the audience, going so far as to forfeit the second game when his complaints weren't addressed. Apparently worn down by Fischer's harping—which some considered to be an attempt to unnerve Spassky—the Russians began making bizarre accusations of their own. They claimed that Fischer had planted a device somewhere on the premises to interfere with Spassky's brain waves. Police officers dismantled Fischer's chair and swept the entire hall in a vain search for such an object.

While these sideshows unfolded, Fischer only got stronger, winning the title handily on September 1. Nine days later, the Russians exacted a measure of revenge, albeit in a different context. In Munich, the Soviets won the Olympic basketball gold medal in the most controversial of circumstances. Trailing the United States by a

1970s

point in the waning seconds, they were given three chances to inbound the ball after a series of curious official rulings, including one by the Secretary General of the International Amateur Basketball Federation, who, technically, had no jurisdiction in the matter. The final attempt ended up in the hands of Aleksandr Belov, who made a layup to give the USSR a 51–50 win. A formal postgame protest by U.S. officials was rejected, and the 12 American players refused to accept their silver medals. They remain unclaimed in an Olympic vault in Switzerland, neglected symbols of the Cold War.

American pro football's best rivalry of the '70s had nothing to do with war (cold or otherwise)—it only seemed that way. For the better part of the decade, the Pittsburgh Steelers and the Oakland Raiders carried on a brutal game of King of the Hill in the American Football Conference. Rivalries often contain at least a trace of moral conflict: there's one good guy, one bad guy. But in the case of the Raiders and the Steelers, everyone wore black.

It all started in 1972. The Steelers had won the teams' regular-season meeting, and were hosting their AFC divisional playoff matchup. The night before the game, dozens of Steelers fans surrounded the Raiders hotel in downtown Pittsburgh. As Oakland tight end Bob Moore made his way past the barricades in place against the tide of Steeler faithful, just trying to return to his room, the cops on duty roughed him up a bit, thinking he was trying to bum rush the hotel. Moore came away from the fracas needing stitches. The game itself was even more wild, as the Steelers won on running back Franco Harris's controversial "Immaculate Reception" in the waning seconds. Bay Area fans will argue to this day that the ball took a deflection off of Pittsburgh running back Frenchy Fuqua—who was leveled by Raiders safety Jack Tatum on the play—before Harris plucked it from the air and scampered 42 yards for a touchdown. The officials ruled that the ball had hit Tatum, not Fuqua, and thus that Harris's

Perennial contenders in the 1970s, Dallas and Pittsburgh met in Super Bowl X and Supe XIII (below), with Pittsburgh winning both times.

Hearst is kidnapped   Streaking sweeps the nation   1975   Saigon falls to the Communists

reception was legal, if not Immaculate.

Oakland and Pittsburgh took turns knocking each other out of the playoffs following the 1973 and '74 seasons, and their annual postseason meeting got nastier in '75. The Raiders showed up at Three Rivers Stadium to find the field frozen solid—owing, according to the groundskeeper, to the fact that the wind had blown a tarp off the field. The Raiders weren't so sure it was an act of Nature. Said running back Pete Banaszak, "[Oakland coach John] Madden asked the groundskeeper, Hey, what happened? The guy kind of winked out of the corner of his eye." (Two years earlier the Steelers had accused the Raiders of soaking the Oakland Coliseum field. They also, at times, accused Oakland of deflating the football, writing obscenities on it and smearing their jerseys with Vaseline.) The Raiders' precision passing attack never got going on the frozen turf, and the Steelers won 16–10. But Pittsburgh paid a price: quarterback Terry Bradshaw was knocked unconscious and Lynn Swann was carried off the field with a concussion.

The ante was upped even higher in their next meeting, the 1976 season opener. Oakland defensive back George Atkinson put a forearm into Swann's head, knocking him out of the game. Afterwards, Noll said Atkinson was part of a "criminal element" that he'd like to see drummed out of the league. Atkinson didn't take to being called a criminal. He sued Noll. At trial, Noll was shown tapes of his own players, and admitted that some of them were just as dirty. (One, Mel Blount, said he would sue his own coach for $5 million.) Noll was ultimately exonerated, but the controversy ratcheted up the tension before their meeting in the AFC Championship game that year. "I have the feeling that the game's been forgotten," said Madden before the game. "It's being treated like World War III."

The Raiders won that game 24–7, but it was the last time in the '70s that they beat the Steelers in the playoffs. Pittsburgh's win over Oakland in 1975 set up a

Thurman Munson (15) and the Yankees collided with the Royals in four American League Championship Series from 1976 to 1980, winning three.

Super Bowl showdown with their other great rivals of the decade, the Dallas Cowboys. Unlike the Raiders, who embraced their outlaw image, the Cowboys saw themselves as good guys. They even had a nickname in line with their white-hatted image: America's Team. "It was much more than a football thing," said Dallas receiver Drew Pearson of the Steelers–Cowboys rivalry. "It was blue-collar versus button-down collar. They hated us for our corporate image and we hated them because they always won."

Indeed, the Steelers won the teams' two Super Bowl matchups. "That whole America's Team thing really irritated us," said Harris many years later. "In our eyes, there was only one America's Team: the Pittsburgh Steelers." But the Steelers weren't the only team in America to annoy their competitors by winning everything in sight. The Yankees won the American League East four times from 1976 to 1980, and all four times they met the Kansas City Royals in the League Championship Series.

Like the Steelers and Cowboys, the Yankees and Royals projected vastly different images. The New York clubhouse was a traveling circus, a state of affairs made most clear when the Yankees' best player, Reggie Jackson, and their manager, Billy Martin, nearly came to blows in the dugout on national television. They bickered and feuded about everything. "Ask two Yankees—especially if one is Martin and the other a player—if the sun is shining and it's even money they will get their stories crossed," wrote Thomas Boswell during the 1977 playoffs.

The Royals, on the other hand, were an affable, agreeable, hardworking and—in direct contrast to the Yankees—humble, bunch. "All baseball wants us to win," said Kansas City manager Whitey Herzog. "Not that they love us ... they just hate the Yankees, and their check-writing."

All of baseball may have wanted Kansas City to win, but the Royals couldn't do it. Chris Chambliss won the 1976 series for the Yankees with a walk-off homer in the decisive fifth game. The '77 series nearly matched the '76

America celebrates its bicentennial 1977 Roots *transfixes the nation* *Elvis Presley dies*

tilt for drama; the '78 series was less climactic—but both ended with the Yankees on top. Beating New York had become, in the words of Royals third baseman George Brett, "the biggest obstacle in our lives." Kansas City finally cleared that obstacle in 1980, when Brett hit a 98-mile-an-hour Goose Gossage fastball into the upper deck in right field at Yankee Stadium in Game 3 of the ALCS. "It was a defining moment for them," Gossage said years later. "Boy, that was a rivalry. I'll never forget those days. Man, that was good, old-fashioned hardball."

Conflicts of all kinds drove most of the 1970s rivalries we've chosen, but one of them demonstrated that it was possible for the participants to simply bring out the best in each other, with little attendant static—and to make spectators feel better just for having seen it. That was the case with the thoroughbreds Affirmed and Alydar, who spent the summer of '78 engaged in one of the most compelling Triple Crown chases in horse racing history.

Affirmed won the first two legs, beating Alydar by 1¼ lengths at the Kentucky Derby and by a neck at the Preakness. The sleek chestnut colt had a chance to win the Triple Crown at the Belmont, but his jockey, Steve Cauthen, had to be especially wary of Alydar, not only because of the rival's performance in the previous two legs, but also because Alydar had handed Affirmed his only two losses (in 15 starts), and both had come at Belmont.

At a mile and a half, the Belmont is the longest of

the three Triple Crown races, and often the toughest to predict, because most horses have little, if any, experience at that distance. The last half-mile can be an unkown quantity. For Affirmed and Alydar, that last half-mile provided the stage for their shining moment. "Anyone who expects that two horses can run in the Kentucky Derby and Preakness and then come back in the Belmont and run head-to-head for the final mile is expecting too much," said trainer Phil Johnson. "But they did it, didn't they?" They did, battling down the stretch, with Cauthen bringing Affirmed home the winner by a head. He was the 11th horse to win the Triple crown; Alydar, with Jorge Velasquez up, was the first to finish second in all three races.

Hall of Fame trainer Woody Stephens was one of many observers to come away breathless. "Been around racing 50 years," he said. "Seen dawn come up over a lot of tracks. Affirmed and Alydar in the Belmont? Probably the best horse race that's ever been run. . . . I'll raise a glass to 'em while I'm watchin' the replays and, damn, I'll root. Come on Affirmed, come on Alydar. Come on Cauthen, come on Velasquez. Whatever it is that these two horses have cannot be bought or manufactured. It's the greatest act horse racing has ever had." Then, summing up what makes a rivalry truly great, he finished his thought. "I hope it never ends."   —M.B.

Disco peaks with the release of Saturday Night Fever   *The first "test-tube" baby is*

Alydar (2) and Velasquez battled Affirmed and Cauthen down to the wire in every race of the 1978 Triple Crown, a stirring series that legendary trainer Woody Stephens called "the greatest act horse racing has ever had."

Lee Trevino (left) picked up in the 1970s where Arnold Palmer left off in the '60s— as the primary rival for the great Jack Nicklaus (above). The alltime leader in major pro titles with 18, Nicklaus nevertheless finished second to Trevino at the 1971 U.S. Open (in a playoff), the '72 British Open (Trevino also won the British in '71) and the 1974 PGA Championship.

The rivalry between the Dallas Cowboys and the Washington Redskins began in 1961, when the teams were first grouped together in the NFL's Eastern Conference, and intensified during the 1970s, when stars like Washington running back John Riggins (44) and Dallas linebacker Thomas (Hollywood) Henderson (top) helped make their teams perennial contenders for the NFC East division title.

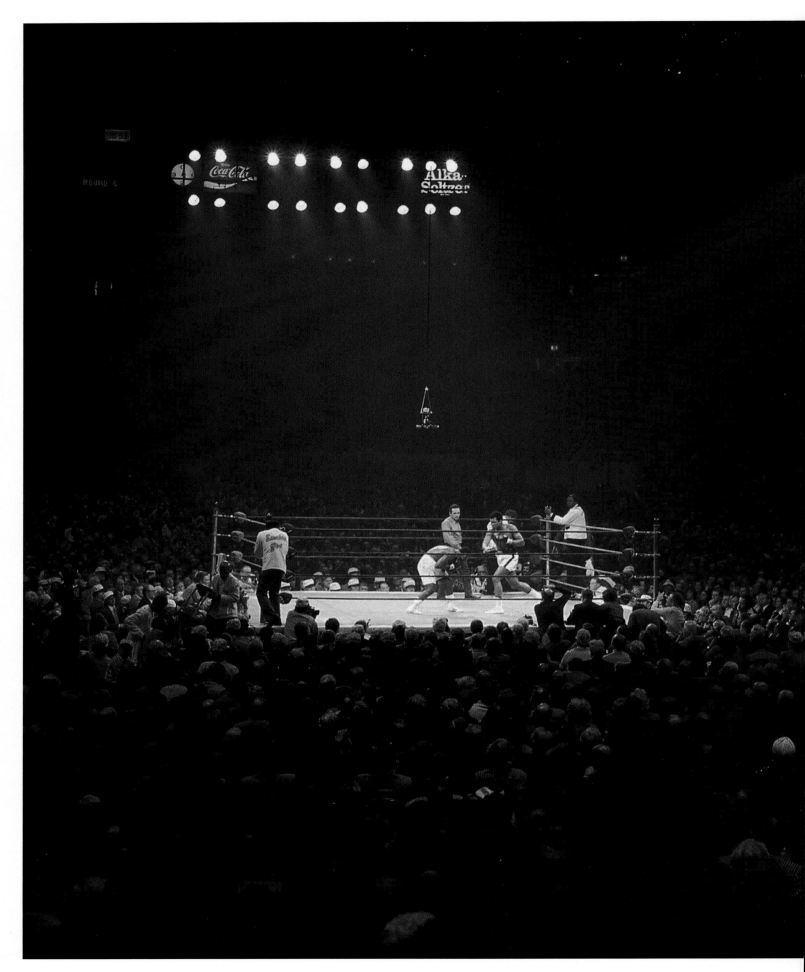

Brad Park of the Boston Bruins (above right) upended Montreal's Jacques Lemaire during the 1978 Stanley Cup finals, but Lemaire's Canadiens dumped the Bruins' title hopes for the second consecutive season, taking the series in six games. It would be the second of three straight championships for Montreal, which swept Park and Boston in the previous year's finals.

Fight fans packed Madison Square Garden for Ali–Frazier II, a non-title bout on Jan. 28, 1974. Ali won a unanimous 12-round decision to avenge his loss in their first meeting, at the same venue, in 1971. The victory earned him a shot at the heavyweight title against George Foreman, who defeated Frazier for the belt in January 1973.

Dallas tight end Jackie Smith (falling) dropped what could have been a game-tying 10-yard touchdown pass from Roger Staubach during the third quarter of Super Bowl XIII against Pittsburgh. The Cowboys had to settle for a field goal, and ended up losing the game 35–31 for their second Super Bowl loss to Pittsburgh in four years.

The Yankees' Willie Randolph absorbed a hard slide from Kansas City's Hal McRae during the 1977 American League Championship Series. For the second year in a row, the teams would need a decisive Game 5 to settle the AL pennant. The Yanks won both series with ninth-inning dramatics, and would take the teams' 1978 ALCS meeting in four games.

Cincinnati Reds catcher Johnny Bench blocked home plate from Ed Ott, his counterpart on the Pittsburgh Pirates, during the 1979 National League Championship Series, in which the Pirates finally took their revenge for NLCS defeats to the Reds in 1970, '72, and '75. Pittsburgh swept the Reds and went on to beat Baltimore in the World Series.

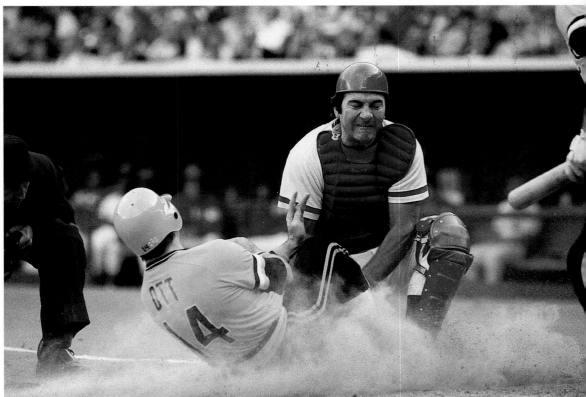

The Rams and Vikings engaged in one of the NFL's great unsung rivalries during the 1970s: Both teams were contenders for most of the decade, and in addition to their regular-season clashes, they met four times in the playoffs, including twice in the NFC title game. Minnesota won three of the four playoff tilts.

Joe Theismann (7) and the Washington Redskins finished 8–8 in 1978, while their archrivals in the NFC East, Dallas, won the division with a 12–4 record and reached Super Bowl XIII. Regardless of the teams' respective standings, though, the Redskins–Cowboys game was always hotly contested, and remains so. Of the 10 division titles up for grabs in the 1970s, Dallas won seven and Washington one (the Redskins also won four wild-card berths). The scales of the rivalry would tip Washington's, and Theismann's, way in the '80s.

A.J. Foyt's turbo-charged Ford (7) unleashed heat waves during a practice run at the 1970 Indianapolis 500. The alltime CART leader in wins with 67, Foyt had several prominent rivals during the 1970s, but perhaps none as fierce as Mario Andretti, who is second on the CART wins list with 52. The two drivers traded the CART season title back and forth through much of the '60s and sustained their rivalry through the 1970s and into the '80s. When Andretti was named Driver of the Year in '78, Foyt answered in '79 with his record seventh CART championship.

The expressions on the faces of this trio of U.S. Olympic basketball players told the story of their team's controversial loss to the Soviet Union in the gold-medal game at the 1972 Games in Munich. The Americans had celebrated victory after Doug Collins sank two free throws to give them a 50–49 lead and the U.S.S.R. had subsequently failed to score on an inbounds play in the final seconds. But a questionable ruling gave the Soviets another possession and more time on the clock, and they scored to win 51–50.

The Steelers–Raiders rivalry of the 1970s was the fiercest in the AFC, if not the entire NFL, and featured such stars as Pete Banaszak (40), and future Hall of Famers Gene Upshaw (63), Mean Joe Greene (75) and Jack Lambert (58). The teams squared off in the AFC title game in 1974, '75 and '76, with Pittsburgh winning the first two meetings and Oakland the third. Each time, the winner went on to Super Bowl glory.

1980s

hn Lennon is murdered Ted Turner's CNN debuts The U.S. boycotts the

TOP 5
NAVRATILOVA–EVERT
JOHNSON–BIRD
LEONARD–DURAN
COE–OVETT
KASPAROV–KARPOV

In the summer of 1984, Converse brough together pro basketball luminaries Larry Joe Bird and Earvin (Magic) Johnson for a commercial shoot at Bird's home in French Lick, Ind. They had eyed each other with a mixture of respect and wariness since facing off on the court for the first time in 1979, when Johnson's Michigan State team downed Bird and Indiana State in the NCAA final. Now, there would be no live audience on hand to observe them, no coaches to direct them, no competition to consume them. They had been rivals for half a decade, but in many ways they were meeting for the first time.

Theirs was not a *mano-a-mano* rivalry; Bird, a 6' 9" small forward, and Johnson, a 6' 9" point guard, seldom covered each other. Their matchup, instead

Not since Chamberlain–Russell had the NBA seen an individual rivalry as compelling as the one between Bird (33) and Magic

elevated their respective *teams* to transcendent levels. Their passing skills and creativity brought everyone on the court into play and made each of their teammates a better player. Only Johnson had a Bird's-eye view of the floor; only Bird approached the mastery of Magic's no-look legerdemain. After entering the NBA in 1979, they joined teams a continent apart—Bird signed with the Boston Celtics, Johnson the Los Angeles Lakers. But soon they were whirling along in a two-step all their own, a left-right, left-right of alternating NBA titles and most valuable player trophies that would propel the league into unprecedented prosperity and their own games to mythic heights.

Before Johnson and Bird joined the NBA, the league's average attendance was 10,822, the average player salary was $148,000, and TV ratings had dropped 26% in a year. By the end of the 1990–91 season, attendance was up to 15,245 per game, the average salary topped $750,000 and three of the league's four most-watched telecasts were Finals games between Bird's Celtics and Johnson's Lakers. "The part I like best is that they added real basketball, they got big money and remained true to the game," said Bill Fitch, Bird's former coach in Boston. "And they've got that great star quality about them. Magic walks into a room and lights it up with his smile. Bird walks in and gives you a little Mark Twain."

Yet for all the sparks Bird and Johnson created on the court and for all the heat of the Boston–Los Angeles rivalry, a deep freeze existed between them at the start of their pro careers. "It was reported in the papers that they didn't like each other," said Magic's agent, Lon Rosen, "and they started to believe it themselves." When Johnson showed up at French Lick for the Con-

Bird's Celtics and Johnson's Lakers won eight of the 10 NBA titles up for grabs in the 1980s. They went head-to-head in three NBA Finals (1984, '85, '87) during the decade, with Los Angeles winning two of those meetings. Magic won three Finals MVP awards and Bird two.

are diagnosed 1982 E.T. *grosses $200 million in 66 days* USA Today *hits the newsstands*

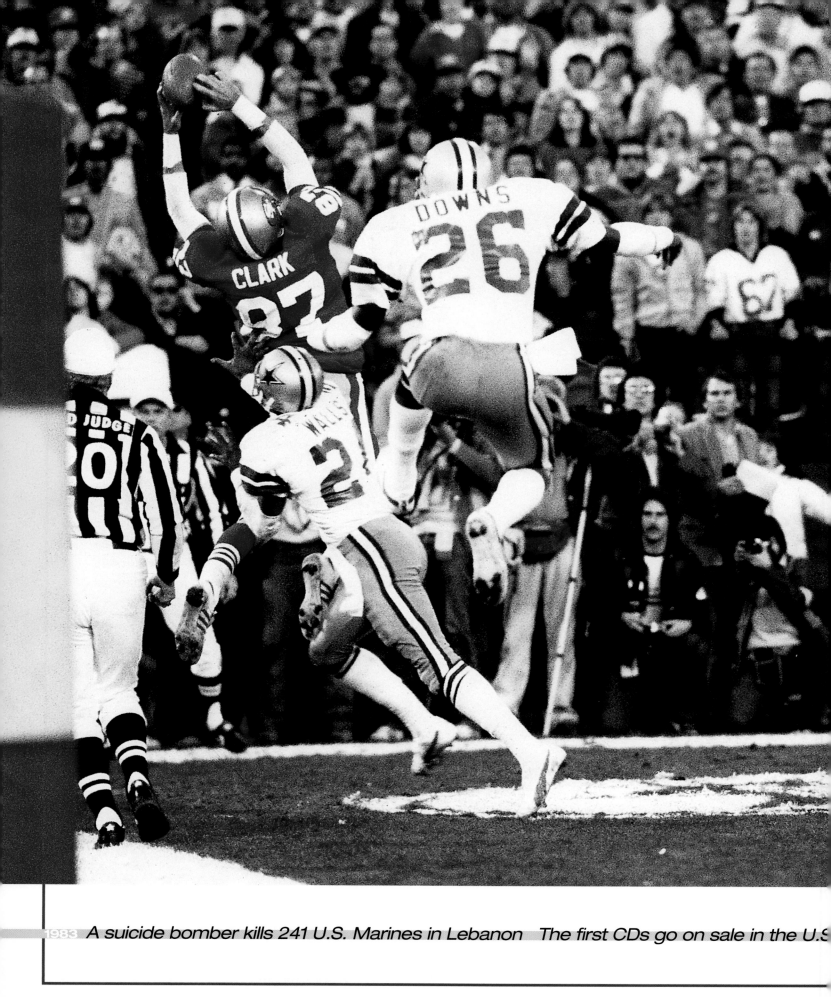

1983 *A suicide bomber kills 241 U.S. Marines in Lebanon   The first CDs go on sale in the U.S.*

Dwight Clark's fingertip grab in the 1981 NFC championship game—forever known as The Catch—not only ended years of futility for San Francisco against its playoff nemesis, Dallas, but also marked a changing of the guard in the NFC.

BY THE NUMBERS

8

Seasons between San Francisco's playoff appearances from 1972 until 1981, a span during which the Cowboys made seven trips to the postseason, advancing to three Super Bowls and winning one championship.

89

Yards—the length of the game-winning, 13-play drive that ended with the Niners' Joe Montana rolling right and hitting Dwight Clark in the back of the Dallas end zone for a six-yard touchdown. The play tied the 1981 NFC championship game at 27–27. Ray Wersching's extra point gave San Francisco the winning margin.

27

Career postseason games played by Dallas linebacker D.D. Lewis, the man in hot pursuit of Montana on the famous scoring play. Lewis's mark would stand as the NFL record until Super Bowl XXXVII in 2003, when Montana's longtime teammate and favorite target, Jerry Rice, played his 28th career postseason game.

35.4

Average points per game for the 49ers against Dallas in five matchups from 1981 to 1989. Dallas averaged 17.6 points a game in the same span. The Cowboys' only win in the series during the '80s came "pre-Catch," in 1980—a 59-14 drubbing at Texas Stadium.

verse ad, Bird had just avenged his NCAA championship game loss to Magic by averaging 27.4 points and 14.0 rebounds in Boston's seven-game conquest of L.A. for the 1984 NBA title. How would Johnson, whose Lakers had won the championship in two of the previous four years, handle this visit to Larry's turf?

Here's how: In no time they were talking easily in Bird's living room, riding three-wheelers around his property and laughing so hard they could barely film the spot. For all of their apparent differences, they realized that each saw himself as a small-town guy with homespun values. In the coming seasons they would chitchat on the court and kick around the notion of co-hosting a fantasy camp. The NBA's marquee foils were, suddenly, friends. "In one sense we're different," Bird said with a smile. "He wants to make $100 million. I only want to make $50 million."

A rivalry distinguishes itself not only by the splendor and intensity of the competition, but also by the psychic charge that exists between the competitors. Put two highly motivated, highly skilled athletes in frequent opposition for high stakes, and there's no telling what kind of relationship they'll forge. The gamut is as wide as the range of games itself: Chess masters have loathed each other, track stars avoided each other, boxers berated each other, tennis stars comforted each other. The good will between Magic and Larry, for instance, did nothing to mute their combativeness on the court. In Game 6 of the 1985 Finals, Magic's triple-double helped the Lakers to a 111–100 victory and gave the franchise its first NBA championship series victory over the Celts in the 38-year history of the Finals. In a pivotal Game 4 two years later, Johnson answered Bird's off-balance three-pointer with a last-second "junior, junior, skyhook" to lead L.A. to a 107–106 win.

"It's the ultimate, beating Boston and Larry,"

1980s

said Magic. "It's special, and it's always going to be special. When we're old, playing checkers and I kick his ass, it's going to be special then, too."

Of course, not all rivalries share such warmth and affection. The NFL's Dallas Cowboys and San Francisco 49ers have had a decidedly cool relationship since 1970, when they first met in the playoffs. The Cowboys won that meeting, denying the 49ers a trip to Super Bowl V, and they would eliminate the Niners from the playoffs the next two seasons as well, setting the stage for the rivalry's peak, after the 1981 season. While the Cowboys continued to contend for championships after those early '70s meetings, reaching Super Bowls VI, X, XII and XIII, San Francisco fell on hard times. The Niner nadir came in 1979, when they went 2–14 for the second consecutive season. But just two years later, under coach Bill Walsh and his young quarterback, Joe Montana, San Francisco finished with the league's best record, going 13–3 and running away with the NFC West title.

After a playoff victory over the Giants, San Francisco once again found Dallas blocking the way to the franchise's first Super Bowl berth. "There was some arrogance about being a Cowboy," said 49ers receiver Dwight Clark. "They came in like they were the established team looking to kick the young upstarts' butts." Dallas coach Tom Landry validated Clark's assessment by saying before the game that "Montana has to be the key. There's nothing else there except him."

It was somewhat ironic, then, that Montana would throw three interceptions and nearly squander his team's brilliant effort in a game that has passed into NFL legend. There were seven lead changes in the pulsating affair, the last coming on one of the most famous plays in league history—Montana's six-yard, game-winning touchdown pass to Clark in the corner of the endzone, now commonly referred to as The Catch. With that, the tide of the rivalry turned, as San Francisco established its own dynasty in the 1980s and Dallas faded.

Britain's Coe (254) and Ovett (279) ruled middle-distance running in the early 1980s; in their eagerly anticipated matchups at the Moscow Games, Ovett took the gold medal in the 800 and Coe won the 1500.

There is another, perhaps more common dynamic in rivalries: unadulterated enmity. Anatoly Karpov was cautious and diplomatic, with fine bones and porcelain skin. Gary Kasparov, 12 years his junior, was brash and outspoken, with the swarthy look of a street fighter. In five matches comprising 144 games over seven years, the two Soviets glared at each other over a chessboard with the world championship on the line. During those countless hours, each knew that a moment's distraction could lead to a mistake that would cost him the one thing he cherished most. "After all the years of seeing the same face, you lose invention," said Andrew Page, Kasparov's manager. "It's like being in a bad marriage."

There was no honeymoon period, either. Kasparov believed he was deprived of a chance to take the title from Karpov in 1984, when the president of the International Chess Federation called off a match after 48 games in 159 days. He finally ended Karpov's decade-long run at the top one year later in Moscow, becoming, at 22, the youngest champion ever.

As each searched for an edge, the tension between them only grew sharper, and weirder. During their 1986 match, an irate Kasparov accused someone in his camp of supplying his game notes to the enemy, while Karpov alleged that a parapsychologist on Kasparov's team was causing turbulence in his brain. The champ held off a furious charge by Karpov to retain his title, then prevailed again the following year in Seville, Spain. After that second successful defense, Kasparov defeated his nemesis one last, all-consuming time, in 1990. "We've played so many times that it's all become one big game to me," Kasparov said. "I cannot separate our matches. . . . It's a lifetime."

Another rivalry from the 1980s featuring two competitors from the same country vying to be the world's best played out on the running tracks of Europe. In one torrid 41-day span in 1979, Britain's Sebastian Coe set world records in the 800, the mile and the 1,500. The following year, Coe's countryman Steve Ovett broke his

The space shuttle Challenger explodes, killing seven   Nintendo's Super Mario Bros. debuts

Leonard (far right) frustrated Duran with his technique, and his showboating, at their historic second bout in New Orleans.

1987 *Jim Bakker's tryst with Jessica Hahn forces him to resign his ministry   Texaco declar*

mile mark and tied his record in the 1,500. All of which meant that as the 1980s dawned, the planet's dominant middle-distance runners came from towns roughly 200 miles apart—Coe from industrial Sheffield, Ovett from the resort of Brighton—yet they rarely found any track on any continent that was mutually suitable for a race.

Though they occasionally volleyed critical remarks about each other through the press, the reasons behind their calculated avoidance were unclear. Some observers cited the benefits each received from running for times rather than victories. "If they go head to head, there's definitely a Number 1," said U.S. runner Tom Byers, "But if they trade world records back and forth, nobody knows." No matter what kept them apart, one event loomed that would surely bring them together: the 1980 Olympics.

Because of the Englishmen's reluctance to face one another, the 800-meter final at Moscow was one of the most eagerly anticipated races in the history of the Games. Coe was favored, but in finishing second to Ovett he took the opportunity to, as he put it later, commit "more cardinal sins of middle-distance running in 1½ minutes than I've done in a lifetime." Ovett expected to achieve a similar result six days later, when they battled in the 1,500, a distance at which (counting its non-metric cousin, the mile) he had not been beaten in 42 straight races. But Coe's finishing kick proved the

BY THE NUMBERS

14

Occasions in which Sweden's Bjorn Borg and John McEnroe of the United States met from 1978 to 1981. The two split those matches evenly, with McEnroe holding an advantage in Grand Slam head-to-heads of three (1980, '81 U.S. Open, 1980 Wimbledon) to one for Borg (1980 Wimbledon).

22

Minutes—duration of the 34-point, fourth-set tiebreaker in the 1980 Wimbledon final, during which McEnroe survived five Borg match points. McEnroe would win 18–16 to knot the match at two sets apiece.

233

Minutes, from start to finish, for the entire five-set match, the longest Wimbledon final since 1954. When it was over, Borg had won his fifth consecutive Wimbledon title in what is widely considered the greatest match in the history of tennis.

5

Number of sets both Borg and McEnroe played in the 1980 semifinals. Borg fell down two sets to none against Johan Kreik before sweeping the final three sets, while McEnroe outlasted Jimmy Connors, winning a fifth-set tiebreaker.

41

Number of consecutive matches—a record—that Borg won at Wimbledon before McEnroe defeated him in the 1981 final. Borg hadn't lost a match at Wimbledon since 1975. Rod Laver holds the second longest streak with 31 straight Wimbledon victories.

greater, and his face bloomed in a mixture of ecstasy and relief as he crossed the finish line in first place. Ovett finished third.

They resumed their rivalry at the next Olympics, but the timing did not bode well for Coe. He arrived in Los Angeles having trained for only seven months after recovering from toxoplasmosis, and even he gave himself little chance. Yet it was Ovett who was done in by illness. Battling bronchitis, a condition exacerbated by the L.A. smog, he had to be taken away on a stretcher after the 800 final, in which Coe won the silver medal. Ovett gamely ran in the 1,500, but 350 yards from the finish he was overcome by chest pains as Coe powered past the field to become the first man to repeat as Olympic 1,500-meter champion.

The war of words before a championship boxing match, uttered to hype the tension and enhance the gate, is often not a clear expression of the fighters' true feelings. Did Roberto Duran really believe it when he said that welterweight champ Sugar Ray Leonard had "no heart" before their June 1980 bout in Montreal? Whether he did or not, Duran's words seemed to find their mark with Leonard. While the experts had expected him to dance against the Panamanian with the legendary *manos de piedra*, Sugar Ray entered the ring furious, combinations flying. Duran withstood those blows and worked inside, pummeling away. For 15 rounds they engaged in a brutal exchange

that rivaled the Ali–Frazier Thrilla in Manila five years earlier. In the end, Duran won a unanimous decision and the crown.

Though Leonard had lost, the way he'd battled put to rest any lingering notions that he was just a pretty boy with fast hands and quick feet. He had gone toe-to-toe with one of the most fearsome fighters in boxing history, revealing himself as not only skilled, but also resourceful and resilient. In the days after the fight, Leonard contemplated retirement at the age of 24. But after a while his resolve hardened; they would fight again in November in New Orleans. "Leonard said he is going to box, move, slip, dance—he's not going to do a damn thing," Duran scoffed. "If he didn't do anything in the first one, he's going to do less in this one."

As the champ boasted, the challenger looked past the hype and envisioned his victory. He believed he only needed to be tactically smarter to win the rematch. In New Orleans, Leonard snapped swift jabs to Duran's head and, when the champion tried to bull his way in, uppercuts to his body. Leonard seized control of the bout, and even began to taunt Duran with showboating maneuvers. With 16 seconds left in the eighth round the unthinkable happened: Unhurt, Duran turned to the referee and said he had had enough. The words he used have dogged him ever since: *No más, no más.*

In a sense, Duran's choice would be mirrored two years later by Sweden's Bjorn Borg: After John McEnroe ended his sublime run of five straight Wimbledon titles, winning a four-set thriller in 1981, a burned-out Borg called it quits in '82. Inspired by his victory over Borg, McEnroe would appear in the next three Wimbledon finals, facing his other great rival of the era, Jimmy Connors, in two of them. Connors won a five-set marathon in 1982, but Johnny Mac would win the next two All-England titles, including a straight-set whipping of Connors in '84.

Chris Evert might have said *no more*

There was no better rivalry during the 1980s than that between Evert (near left) and Navratilova, who met 80 times during their legendary careers.

as well in the early 1980s, when Martina Navratilova took the upper hand of their rivalry. Evert had, after all, dominated to that point, winning 20 of 25 matches since their initial meeting, in 1973. But Navratilova turned the tables, at one point winning 13 in a row over Evert. Still, Evert, the elder by almost two years, battled on, breaking through on rare occasions. When she finally did retire they had faced each other 80 times in 15 years—including 14 times in Grand Slam finals. For 12 consecutive years, from 1975 through '86, one or the other finished the season ranked No. 1 in the world.

They were from two different worlds, and their games stood in glorious contrast. Evert was a steel-nerved surgeon along the baseline, groomed for greatness in the Florida sunshine. Navratilova was an explosive serve-and-volleyer from Czechoslovakia who grew up pining for a more open life in America. By the time of the 1975 U.S. Open, they had grown friendly enough that Chris was one of the few people who knew what Martina had planned. After Chris beat her 6–4, 6–4 in the semis, Navratilova went to Manhattan and defected.

Over the years, they grew closer, consulting each other on schedules, checking with the source on any personal remarks in the press the other was alleged to have made, having ad hoc heart-to-hearts. They dressed together before matches and afterward returned to the same locker room to shower and occasionally put on makeup, sometimes side by side. "When you think about it, when Martina and I play, we're there, before and after, stripped of everything—literally naked," Evert said. "But more than that, we've both seen each other so vulnerable. We've seen each other hurt and crying."

Yet never once after a tough loss did one ask the other to leave her alone. They may have competed for hours, knowing that one's exaltation would be the other's pain, yet that knowledge didn't drive them apart. It made them better friends and better rivals.   —H.H.

Jimmy Connors (left) won two of the first five U.S. Opens of the 1980s, while McEnroe won three. They met in two Wimbledon finals during the decade, with Connors taking a five-setter in 1982, and McEnroe winning in straight sets in '84.

One year after their epic 1980 Wimbledon final, which is often referred to as the greatest match in tennis history, Borg and McEnroe met again for the title at the All-England Club. This time, McEnroe (near court) prevailed in four sets (two of them going to a tiebreaker) and ended Borg's five-year reign at Centre Court.

Teammates at the 1981 Ryder Cup in Surrey, England, Tom Watson (crouching) and Jack Nicklaus had been archrivals at the Mas-

ters earlier that year as Watson won his second green jacket and Nicklaus finished runner-up along with Johnny Miller.

The New York Rangers–New York Islanders rivalry, which endures today, had its heyday in the 1980s, when Bryan Trottier (above left) and the Islanders ruled the NHL, winning four straight Stanley Cup titles. Mike Allison (right) and the Rangers scrapped mightily to derail the Isles' "Drive for Five" in 1984, but lost in overtime in the deciding fifth game of a tense first-round playoff series. The Islanders reached the Stanley Cup finals, where they were stopped at last by the Edmonton Oilers.

In a thoroughbred matchup that rivaled the legendary Alydar–Affirmed series of 1978, Sunday Silence (8) and Easy Goer finished 1–2 in every Triple Crown race of 1989. Sunday Silence took the Kentucky Derby and the Preakness, with Easy Goer finishing a close second both times before turning the tables and running away with the Belmont by eight lengths.

The rivalry between Carl Lewis of the U.S. and Ben Johnson of Canada, which began in 1980, became increasingly hostile as Lewis (second from right) hinted that Johnson's astounding performances were suspicious, a suggestion that proved well-founded at the '88 Olympics, where Johnson (right) tested positive for steroids.

Broncos defensive back Louis Wright (20) made an interception against the Raiders during Denver's 17–14 overtime loss in 1985, the Broncos' second OT loss to the Raiders that year. Through the 2002 season, the AFC West foes had met 87 times, with Oakland winning 52 of those games.

Dallas defensive end Harvey Martin (left, 79) closed in on San Francisco quarterback Joe Montana during the famous 1981 NFC title game. Montana's thrilling game-winning touchdown pass to Dwight Clark in the waning seconds canceled out the three interceptions he threw during the game.

Chris Evert (above) lost the U.S. Open final to Martina Navratilova in 1984, a year in which she appeared in every Grand Slam final, dropping three of them to her famous archrival.

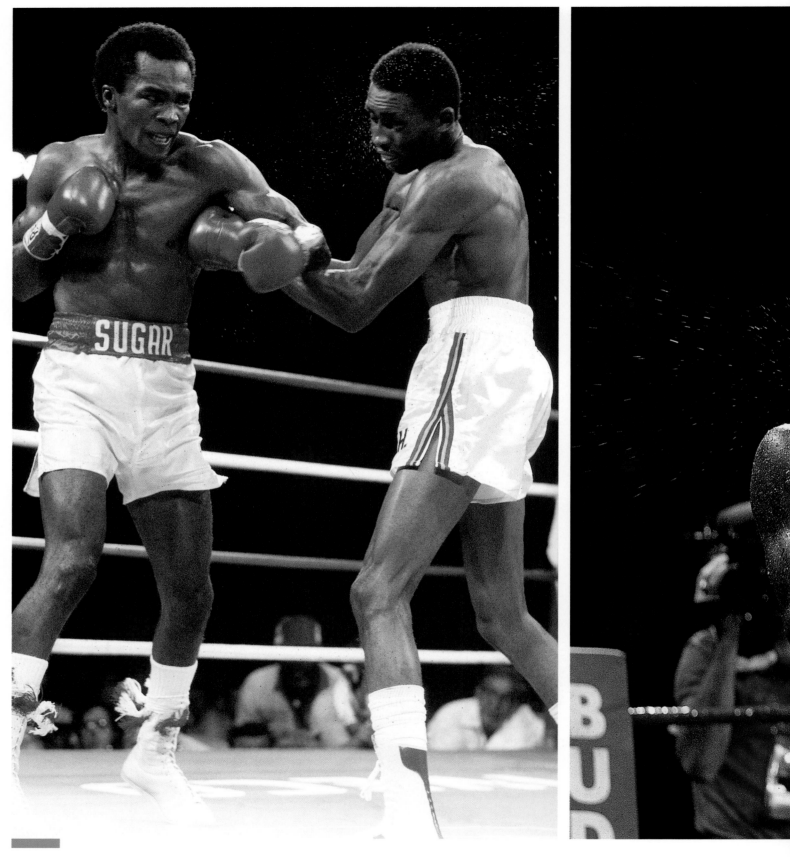

With fierce determination showing on his face, Sugar Ray Leonard shed his finesse tactics and outslugged Thomas Hearns for the WBA and WBC welterweight titles in 1981. Ring magazine named the bout Fight of the Year.

Leonard and Hearns bookended the 1980s with stirring title fights, meeting as welterweights in 1981 and as super middle-weights eight years later. Leonard came from behind to win the first bout, stopping Hearns with a furious flurry in the 14th round, and retained his WBC title in the second bout (above), earning a contro-versial draw despite being knocked down twice in the 12-rounder.

1990s and Beyond

TOP 5

RED WINGS–AVALANCHE
KNICKS–HEAT
DUKE–NORTH CAROLINA
ENGLAND–ARGENTINA
LAKERS–KINGS

A number of fledgling rivalries took flight during the 1990s, several of them involving franchises and athletes that were themselves mere hatchlings. For instance, the NHL's Colorado Avalanche didn't exist before 1995—or more accurately, they existed as the Quebec Nordiques—but when they came into being that year, and were plunked into the same conference as the Detroit Red Wings, an intense rivalry was instantly born. And we mean instantly. In their first home game, on Oct. 6, the Avalanche squared off against the Detroit Red Wings in a rough-and-tumble affair that saw Colorado kill off nine Detroit power plays to win 3–2. The close scoreline and overflowing penalty boxes set the tone for what would quickly

Detroit's Martin Lapointe collided with Sandis Ozolinsh of Colorado during a typically physical moment in the 1990s' nastiest NHL rivalry.

1990s

grow into the fiercest NHL rivalry of the decade.

Both teams finished atop their divisions that season, and they wound up meeting in the Western Conference finals, with a trip to the Stanley Cup finals at stake. In the first period of Game 3 of that series, Detroit's Slava Kozlov slammed Colorado defenseman Adam Foote face-first into the glass. No penalty was called, but Foote was left with a gash on his forehead that required 20 stitches to close. (In true hockey-player form, a stitched-up Foote returned to the game in the second period—and scored a goal.)

Kozlov's hit didn't sit well with Colorado's Claude Lemieux, who took it upon himself to extract a measure of revenge, which he did by sucker punching Kozlov in the mouth, a move that, in turn, provoked the ire of Detroit coach Scotty Bowman. Bowman waited in the parking lot for Lemieux after the game, which the Avalanche won 6–4, and when Lemieux emerged with his wife and two-month-old son, the 62-year-old Bowman rained verbal abuse down on him. (We said this rivalry was hot-blooded; we didn't say it was always classy.)

Lemieux's shot at Kozlov may have evened the score, but the score didn't stay that way for long. Six days later, in Game 6, Lemieux checked Red Wings forward Kris Draper into the boards from behind. Draper ended up with a broken cheekbone, a fractured jaw and nose, a handful of bro-

BY THE NUMBERS

5
Occasions on which the Red Wings and Avalanche have met in the Western Conference playoffs. All of their matchups occurred after 1995, and three times the winner of the series went on to win the Stanley Cup.

$1,000
Amount Claude Lemieux was fined for cross checking Detroit's Kris Draper into the boards during the 1996 Western Conference finals, stoking the flames of the rivalry. Draper suffered severe facial lacerations and a fractured jaw. In addition to the fine, Lemieux was suspended for the first two games of the 1996 Stanley Cup finals.

148
Penalty minutes, including 18 major penalties for fighting, in the Red Wings–Avalanche game of March 26, 1997, when the Wings appeared to be exacting retribution for the Draper injury the previous season. Goaltenders Mike Vernon and Patrick Roy got into the act as well, squaring off during a first-period melee that delayed the game for 10 minutes.

0
Number of players and coaches fined or suspended by the NHL for taking part in the March 26, 1997, brawl.

5
Stanley Cup titles won by the two teams from 1996 to 2002. From 1996 to '98 Detroit and Colorado went a combined 12–0 in games against the Eastern Conference champions in the Finals. The only other teams to win the Stanley Cup since 1996 were the Dallas Stars (2000) and the New Jersey Devils (2001).

ken teeth and 30 stitches on his face. To add insult to multiple facial injuries, the Avalanche closed out the series with a 4–1 win in that game. Lemieux was suspended for the first two games of the '96 Stanley Cup, in which Colorado defeated Florida.

The teams' first meeting the following season passed without incident, but at the second, tempers started to rise. Colorado's Alexei Gusarov and Rene Corbet ended up with concussions, and following the game, which the Avalanche won 4–3, Colorado general manager Pierre Lacroix got into a heated shouting match with Red Wings assistant coaches Barry Smith and Dave Lewis, accusing Detroit players of taking cheap shots. Bowman, meanwhile, was busy griping about the visitors' benches at McNichols Sports Arena.

Claiming they are too cramped, Bowman had a carpenter build a portable addition to the bench that the team took with it when it traveled to the Rockies. All of the ill will boiled over during the teams' final regular-season meeting, on March 26, 1997. It was Lemieux's first game in Detroit since his hit on Draper. "It was really bad," Lemieux said later. "We were get-ting faxes from Detroit threatening my life. I had to go in under a fake name. I had a security guy sleeping outside my room in the hotel, following me wherever I went. It got out of control. I wasn't prepared for that game."

The flashpoint of the Colorado–Detroit rivalry came during Game 6 of the 1996 Western Conference finals, when the Avalanche's Claude Lemieux (foreground) crumpled the Red Wing's Kris Draper with an illegal hit, breaking several bones in his face.

Detroit forward Darren McCarty dropped his gloves and went after Lemieux in the first period. Lemieux did little to enhance his image; he quickly dropped to the ice and covered himself as best he could while McCarty pounded him until the referees skated in to break it up. The rest of the game looked like an outtake of *Slap Shot*, with even the goalies squaring off at one point.

According to Detroit forward Brendan Shanahan, McCarty's beating of Lemieux changed the course of the season. "That game helped make us a team," said Shanahan. "We felt we were growing as a group, but that game gave us—and everyone else—a visual picture. We knew how we felt about sticking up for each other, but that was the opportunity we had to show it."

The teams met again in the Western Conference finals, and when Detroit won the series in six games there was no downplaying the significance of the slugfest

on March 26. Following that game, the Red Wings went 19-7-3, while the Avalanche finished 13–11. The Conference final itself, of course, featured a fair amount of mayhem. In the third period of Game 4 alone there were 204 penalty minutes, and Shanahan battered Rene Corbet, whom he outweighed by 30 pounds, in a fight. Yet that was not as shameful as the 6'1", 215-pound Lemieux picking on the 5'10", 185-pound Kozlov during a scrum and then skating away whenever the Red Wings' 6'2", 210-pound defenseman Bob Rouse moved in. Given displays like this from Lemieux, it came as a bit of a surprise the following fall when, in the teams' first meeting of the 1997–98 season, Lemieux, a right wing, asked left wing Jeff Odgers to switch places with him just before the opening faceoff at Joe Louis Arena. The switch put Lemieux directly across from McCarty. Unbeknownst to McCarty and the rest of the Red Wings, Lemieux had been taking lessons from Avalanche enforcer Francois Leroux, and he jumped McCarty as soon as the puck hit the ice. "I'm not going to hire a bodyguard," Lemieux said. "I can take care of myself. A lot of our guys fought their hearts out for me in [the March 26] game, and that was my payback."

After the game McCarty grudgingly admitted that Lemieux's actions earned him a little respect. "It would have been easy for him to let things lie as they were," he said. But he stopped short of expressing admiration. "In my mind he's still an idiot because he still hasn't apologized to [Draper]. I have no respect for a person who doesn't take responsibility for his actions."

For a change, the teams didn't meet in the playoffs in 1998, when the Wings won their second straight Stanley Cup. But Detroit's run was ended the following year by—who else?—the Avs, and the two met

again in the playoffs in 2000 and 2002, proving that the hottest rivalry in sports showed no signs of cooling off. And though we've focused on the brawling, it's mainly the quality of the hockey that these two teams play that makes their rivalry the best in sports at the moment. With superstars like Peter Forsberg, Brett Hull, Joe Sakic, Chris Chelios and Patrick Roy, the Wings and Avalanche both rank among the elite teams in NHL history.

The NBA's top rivalry of the decade was similar to the Avalanche-Red Wings drama—it involved an established team, a new team, and a lot of scrapping, though not as much talent and quality play. The Miami Heat joined the

1993 *49 consecutive days of rain produce the worst flooding in Midwestern history*

NBA in 1988, but they were never more than a mediocre team until the 1995–96 season, when they hired Pat Riley to be their head coach and president. Riley had spent the previous four seasons with the Knicks, bringing them within a game of the 1994 NBA championship.

When he abandoned New York for Miami, the Knicks refused him permission to take Jeff Van Gundy, one of his assistants, with him. Van Gundy suggested to Riley that he hire his brother Stan, which Riley did. The Knicks hired Don Nelson as coach, but he lasted only 59 games. With no better option, New York president Dave Checketts turned to Van Gundy to coach the final 23 games of the season. Van Gundy went

13–10 and guided the Knicks to a first-round playoff sweep of Cleveland. Checketts removed the word "interim" from Van Gundy's job title.

Aside from Knicks fans booing Riley when he returned to New York, there was little bad blood between the two teams—until May of 1997, when they met in the second round of the Eastern conference play-offs. In Game 5, Miami's 6'11" forward P.J. Brown, claiming that Knicks point guard Charlie Ward was about to low-bridge him, flung the 6'1" Ward over his hip and over the baseline, touching off the first of many Miami–New York brouhahas. Before Game 6, the Van Gundy brothers spoke on the phone.

Kurt Cobain commits suicide   Seinfeld reaches No. 1 in the Nielsen ratings

BY THE NUMBERS

19

Combined number of Tar Heels and Blue Devils taken in the first round of the NBA draft from 1990 to '99. Twelve of those players were lottery picks and one, Elton Brand, was selected first overall (in 1999). In all, the two schools have produced 54 first-round selections.

2

Times during the 1990s that Duke and North Carolina met when they were ranked as the top two teams in the nation. The games, which took place on Feb. 3, 1994, and Feb. 5, 1998, featured No. 1 Duke visiting No.2 North Carolina at Chapel Hill. The second-ranked Tar Heels won both meetings.

10

Combined Final Four appearances by Duke and North Carolina during the 1990's. Duke won two national championships during the decade and were runners-up twice; North Carolina won the 1993 national title.

11

Miles on North Carolina highway 15-501 that separate Duke University, in Durham, and the University of North Carolina in Chapel Hill.

30 feet

Distance of the shot that Duke's Jeff Capel made at the end of the first overtime on Feb. 2, 1995, to tie a game against UNC. With coach Mike Krzyzewski sidelined by back surgery, the downtrodden Blue Devils started the ACC season at 1–7, but put up a valiant fight against Jerry Stackhouse, Rasheed Wallace and the rest of the Tar Heels. Donald Williams got hot in the second overtime period, leading North Carolina to a 102–100 win.

1995 The terrorist bombing of a federal office building in Oklahoma City kills 169   O.J. Simpso

After they exchanged pleasantries, Stan said, "I can't believe what Charlie Ward did." "Forget Charlie Ward!" Jeff yelled. "P.J. Brown, that mother----ing coward!" They continued in this vein for a few more minutes before Jeff slammed down the phone. The Knicks and the Heat played a hotly contested postseason series in each of the next three years—all of them went the distance—and each year Stan and Jeff decided not to speak during those weeks. In fact, their parents stopped attending New York–Miami games. They watched at home, with Bill, their father, in one room with the sound down and their mother, Cindy, in another with the volume turned up.

The rivalry was no less intense for the players. Fights broke out regularly. "It's something about them," Heat point guard Tim Hardaway said. "Every time they get down, they want to fight or push and shove and get you going like Dennis Rodman–type guys. You know it's coming." In 1998, Alonzo Mourning and Larry Johnson got into a fight in the waning seconds of Game 4, a 90–85 Knicks victory. Jeff Van Gundy left the bench to try to break it up, and ended up clutching the 7-foot Mourning's lower leg like a kindergartner begging his mom not to leave him alone at school. Every year they expected to meet in the playoffs. "They want us, we want them," Knicks forward Marcus Camby said in 2000. "It's the kind of thing where the Knicks and Miami meet every year. The games are so intense and close. Everyone is going to want to watch this series." The Knicks won three of their four consecutive playoff meetings, which were invariably low-scoring, defensive affairs.

College basketball's best rivalry during the 1990s featured not an upstart against an established team but a pair of longstanding blue-chip programs from the same state—Duke and North Carolina. Remarkably, one or both of the two Tobacco Road teams reached the Final Four in every year of the decade except '96. In '91 both schools made it, and from '91 to 2001 the

The Duke–North Carolina rivalry enjoyed a golden age in the '90s, producing a bevy of future pros such as Christian Laettner (32) and Eric Montross (00).

ACC powers won four national championships.

As the new millennium dawned in the NBA, an intense rivalry rose in the West, between the Kings and the Lakers. These teams, too, shared striking similarities with other great rivalries of the decade. Like the Knicks (and the Red Wings), the Lakers were an established power with a brash coach. Like the Heat (and the Avalanche), the Kings were a relatively young team. They moved from Kansas City to Sacramento in 1985, and were one of the league's more anonymous franchises until late in the 1990s. The Kings made the playoffs as an eighth seed in 2000, which meant they would face the Lakers in the first round.

Only 400 miles from L.A., Sacramento is light years away from the City of Angels in terms of glamour and reknown. If its inhabitants had an inferiority complex, Los Angeles coach Phil Jackson certainly fed it during the 2000 playoffs, saying the populace was "semi-civilized" and "those people are just rednecks in some form or fashion." Jackson may have been playing around, but Kings fans didn't take kindly to his remarks, and they responded with a spirited display of civic pride, elements of which included the burning of purple-and-gold jerseys, the use of electronic noisemakers behind the visitors' bench and the ringing of cowbells throughout their Arco Arena.

The Lakers won a tight five-game series, which had Jackson feeling especially chippy when he returned to Sacramento for the first time during the 2000–01 season. When asked what type of reception he was expecting, Jackson complimented the fans, saying, "Arco Arena is home to a great home crowd, that's their team, their game, the one game in town." With that last remark lingering at the edge of put-down territory, Jackson plunged ahead. "Besides, what else do they play? Pick the fruits and vegetables?"

The Lakers knocked the Kings out of the playoffs again in 2001, sweeping them in the second round. In

1998 *Monica Lewinsky becomes a household name* *Online Christmas-season commerc*

2002, Sacramento passed Los Angeles in the standings, winning the Pacific Division by three games. The teams met in the Western Conference finals and Sacramento took a two-games-to-one lead. The Kings led by 24 points in the second quarter of Game 4, and by eight with less than four minutes to play. The Lakers rallied and won the game in dramatic fashion on Robert Horry's buzzer-beating three-pointer.

O'Neal (near left), Kobe Bryant (8) and the Lakers denied Vlade Divac and the Kings in the 2002 Western Conference finals, then rubbed it in.

"Honestly, it was terrible," said Sacramento's personnel director, Jerry Reynolds. "It's one of those things where for two weeks, I just pouted like a child. And then, about the time I got over it, I realized how much money it had cost me. I just think it's one of those things you never get over 'cause we felt like we should have won the series."

But they didn't. Having evened the series at two games apiece, the Lakers went on to win it in seven, albeit after a highly controversial Game 6, a 106–102 Lakers victory in which the referees whistled Sacramento for 27 fouls in the fourth quarter and Los Angeles for just nine, prompting—no kidding—Ralph Nader to call for an official investigation. After the clamor died down, the Lakers had still won the series, and they didn't let Sacramento forget it. In the offseason, Shaquille O'Neal referred to the team as "the Queens," producing even more bad blood, which boiled over in a 2003 preseason brawl between Sacramento swingman Doug Christie and Lakers forward Rick Fox. A few months later, O'Neal took another shot at the Kings, questioning the inclusion of Sacramento's Mike Bibby on the 2004 U.S. Olympic team. "How did Mike Bibby get on the team?" Shaq asked. "Any Cub Scout with Boy Scouts can do Boy Scoutish things. When [Bibby] was in the Cub Scouts, he was a Cub Scout. When he was with Vancouver, nobody heard about [him]."

A few nights later, Shaq scored his 20,000th career point at Arco Arena. During a timeout in the fourth quarter, someone at courtside grabbed the ball, which had been set aside as a memento for O'Neal, and scrawled "Shaq, you're an a------" on it. No one noticed until after the game, which led to thinly veiled accusations from O'Neal that someone from the Kings had defaced his keepsake.

The premier rivalry in women's tennis also featured a young upstart challenging a more established star, though in this case both participants came from the same family. Venus Williams was the first of the Williams sisters to win two Grand Slam tournaments in one season, but when Venus's younger sister Serena came into her own, the tables quickly turned—for Venus as well as for the rest of women's tennis. The Williams sisters met each other in the finals of four of five Grand Slam events beginning with the 2001 U.S. Open. (Serena won three of them, losing only their first meeting.) But this rivalry had one crucial difference from our other '90s matchups: While, say, the Kings and Lakers had no problem getting up for their head-to-head meetings, the Williams sisters dreaded playing one another. There was something anticlimactic about their meetings—even though they were clearly the class of the women's game. "I'm always the big sister," said Venus after a rare win over Serena. "I always take care of Serena, no matter what. I always make the decisions. I'm always a role model for Serena. I'm the big sister. I always worry about her." Perhaps this mindset undercut the competitiveness of their meetings; in any case, Serena, who won three of the four majors in 2002, can clearly take care of herself.

While the Williams sisters are fast establishing themselves on a plane above their competition, there are some rivalries in this era that transcend sports. The England–Argentina soccer saga falls into this category. In 1986, four years after the two countries went to war in the Falkland Islands, Argentina and England met in the World Cup quarterfinals. In the space of four minutes at at the beginning of the second half, Argentina's Diego Maradona scored the most infamous and most famous

goals in World Cup history. The first one came when he leaped toward a ball in front of the England goalkeeper, Peter Shilton, and appeared to punch it over the 'keeper with his fist. The ball sailed into the net, and Maradona celebrated as if he had headed it in. He fooled the referee, who let the goal stand. Replays clearly showed that it was a handball, though, and Maradona offered the cheeky explanation that the goal had come from "the hand of God." But his next goal, just three minutes later, was

truly divine. Maradona collected the ball in midfield and dashed 60 yards with it, dribbling around three England defenders, and Shilton, before slotting the ball home to give Argentina a 2–0 lead and an eventual 2–1 victory. FIFA later named it the best goal in the World Cup's history.

Twelve years later, Argentina downed England in another World Cup quarterfinal, taking the game on penalty kicks after England midfielder David Beckham was red-carded for kicking Diego Simeone. Beckham hardly touched Simeone, but it was a retaliatory action, and the Argentine player made a meal of it, flopping to the ground dramatically and drawing the card. Beckham was villified in the British press for his mistake.

The next World Cup meeting between England and

Argentina, at the 2002 tournament in Korea and Japan, was one of the most anxiously awaited soccer games in England's history. Nearly one in five English workers took the day off to watch the game, costing the English economy $2.55 billion. But all of those workers, and perhaps the nation's treasury officials, would agree that it was worth it, as Beckham scored the game's only goal on a 44th-minute penalty kick, giving England the revenge it had been waiting to extract for 16 years. "The penalty was probably the sweetest moment in my career because, as I said before, this game meant so much to me, and to my family, and to the whole nation," Beckham said. "As a footballing nation, we've been waiting for that result for a long time."

Argentina's Roberto Ayala (2) upended Michael Owen of England during the teams' meeting at the 1998 World Cup in France. Owen scored one of the best goals of the tournament in the game, which Argentina won on penalty kicks.

Indeed, Queen Elizabeth II, not known for her passion for sports, was given updates on the match as she visited an agricultural show in southern England. Prince William and Prince Harry watched at their country home in western England, and prime minister Tony Blair also tuned in. Only Prince Charles missed the game, as he was busy touring Sicily. When greeted by well-wishers, the future king of England had only one question for them: "Why aren't you watching the football?"

In 1992, Florida State kicker Dan Mowrey (9) missed a 39-yard field-goal attempt that would have tied Miami on the game's final play at the Orange Bowl, pushing the ball to the right of the goal posts. It was the second straight year that the Seminoles had fallen to the Hurricanes in a pivotal game after missing a field-goal attempt wide right. When it happened again in 2000, the game was dubbed Wide Right III.

Frankie Hejduk of the U.S. (above left) challenged Mexico's Rafael Garcia for a head ball during the 1999 U.S. Cup in San Diego. The dramatic improvement of the U.S. team during the 1990s boosted the rivalry, which reached a peak in the 2002 World Cup, where the Yanks eliminated Mexico in the Round of 16.

Future teammates at Manchester United, Argentina's Juan Veron (11) and England's David Beckham (7) were fierce rivals at France '98; Beckham, who would be infamously red-carded in the match, achieved a measure of redemption at the 2002 Cup in Korea/Japan.

Tennessee's Teresa Geter (left, 40) and Michelle Snow (00) converged on Connecticut's Tamika Williams during a January 1999 game in Storrs, Conn. Arguably the two most dominant teams in NCAA women's basketball history, the Lady Vols and the Huskies met for the national title in 1995, 2000 and 2003 with UConn winning all three championships; Tennessee has won six titles since 1987, including three in a row from 1996 to '98.

As classic as the teams' royal blue and powder blue uniforms, the Duke–North Carolina rivalry burned brightest during the 1990s, when it featured such future NBAers as Christian Laettner, Jerry Stackhouse, Grant Hill, Brendan Haywood (00, receiving a pass from Kris Lang), Elton Brand (center) and Corey Maggette (50). One or both teams reached the NCAA Final Four in every year of the decade except 1996.

Brazil's Ayrton Senna readied himself for the start of the Phoenix Grand Prix in 1991, the year that one of Senna's chief rivals, Michael Schumacher, burst onto the Formula 1 circuit. Senna would go on to win the Phoenix Grand Prix as well as the season title that year with his other great rival, France's Alain Prost, finishing second in both competitions.

Michael Schumacher cornered tightly at the 1992 San Marino Grand Prix in Imola, the track where, two years later, Senna would tragically lose his life, depriving F1 of a rivalry that, given more time, might have grown into the greatest in the sport's history. Following Senna's death, Schumacher replaced the Brazilian as the dominant driver on the circuit, winning five titles in nine years.

Friends and rivals since 1990, Pete Sampras (above left) and Andre Agassi met in the final of the 1999 ATP world championship in Germany. The two have played each other in the finals of every major but the French Open, most recently meeting for the 2002 U.S. Open title, which Sampras took 6–3, 6–4, 5–7, 6–4.

Annika Sorenstam of Sweden (above left) and Australia's Karrie Webb became spirited rivals during the '90s, with one of them being named Player of the Year in each season from 1997 to 2002. Based on her dominant performances in 2001 and '02, Sorenstam moved in front, but Webb still led 6–4 in major titles won.

Serena (foreground) and Venus Williams have developed an intriguing, if somewhat reluctant, rivalry as they have come to thoroughly dominate women's tennis. The sisters met in the finals of the 2001 and '02 U.S. Opens, and played in three of the four Grand Slam finals of 2002, with Serena winning all three.

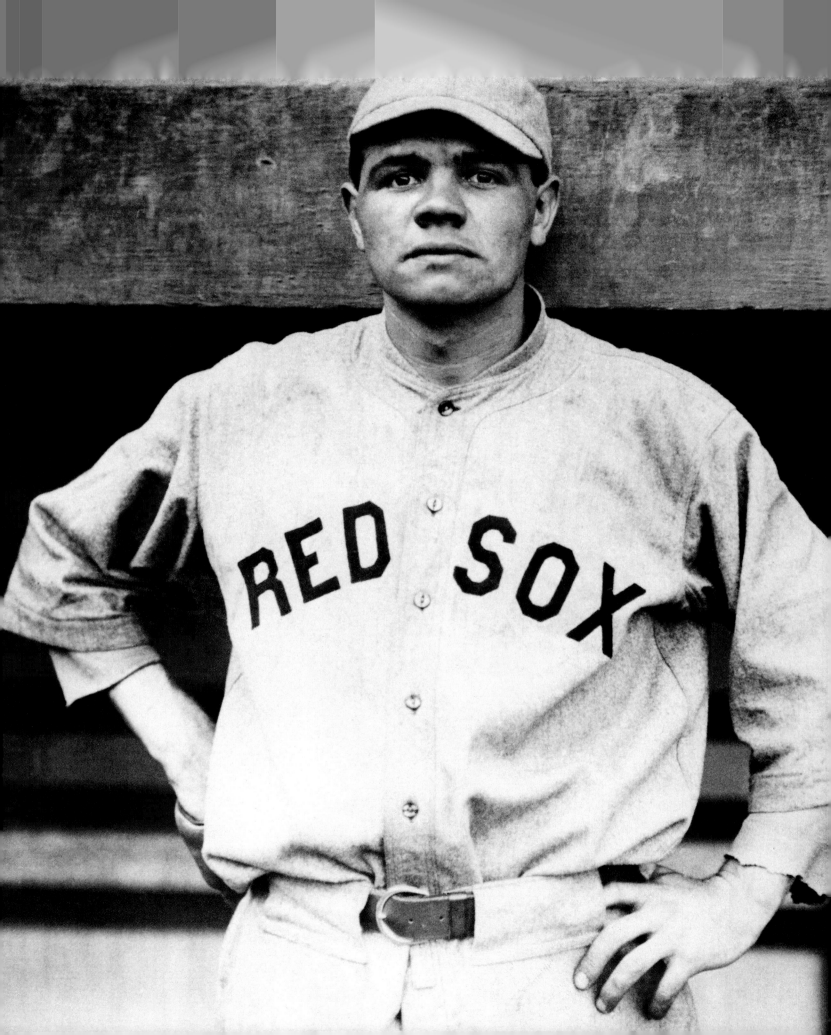

Archrivals

What is arguably the greatest rivalry in sports might never have been hatched if not for the financial entanglements of a

TOP 4

YANKEES–RED SOX
OHIO STATE–MICHIGAN
LAKERS–CELTICS
CELTIC–RANGERS

New York theatrical figure. Before 1919, the Boston Red Sox were riding high, having won three of the previous four World Series. The man paying the team's bills was Harry Frazee, a Broadway mogul who bought the Sox in 1916. The star of his team was Babe Ruth, who hit 29 home runs in 1919, a major-league record total and 19 more than his nearest competitor in the American League. In addition to being baseball's best player, Ruth was the game's biggest draw, and he wanted a larger-than-life salary to accommodate his larger-than-life lifestyle. He asked Frazee for $20,000 a season, but the Broadway impresario, whose venture into baseball complicated his finances and strained his credit, didn't want to give it up.

Ruth began his career in 1914 with the Red Sox, who famously—or infamously, to Boston fans—dealt him to New York in 1919.

Frazee's office on West 45th Street in New York

York was just a few blocks from the office of Col. Jacob Ruppert, owner of the Yankees. In the winter of 1919, Ruppert and his partners approached Frazee and they reached an agreement that sent Ruth to the Yankees. "The price was something enormous, but I do not care to name the figures," said Frazee. (It was $100,000 in cash, plus a $300,000 loan to pay the mortgage on Fenway Park.) "I should have preferred to have taken players in exchange for Ruth, but no club could have given the amount the Yankees have paid for him, and I do not mind saying I think they are taking a gamble."

Ruth took batting practice before a game against Boston in 1926, a season in which he hit .372 with a league-leading 47 home runs and 146 RBIs.

Maybe it was those famous last words that sealed the fate of Frazee's team. Perhaps if the Boston owner hadn't made such a laughably wrong-headed assessment of what would turn out to be *the* landmark transaction in the histories of both franchises, Red Sox fans would not *still* be waiting for a championship, 84 years later. But he did, and they are, while the Yankees, who had not won a pennant to that point, took the American League flag six times in the next nine years and went on to become baseball's most dominant team. After jettisoning Ruth, the Red Sox finished last in eight of the next 11 years. Frazee became the least popular man in the Hub. (He had a successful play called *My Lady Friends*, prompting one Beantown local to grouse, "They're the only friends the sonofabitch has.") In addition to the owner, fans blamed the team's descent on darker forces; it felt like a curse—the Curse of the Bambino, a spell that would be invoked countless times in the next eight decades, as Boston's title drought stretched into the 21st century.

Since that epochal trade, the teams have been forever entwined, but with almost comically—if not cosmically—one-sided results. The Yanks have won, at last count, 26 World Series titles; the Sox, as we've said, none (since 1918). And the teams have played each other numerous times every season since both franchises were established, resulting in a bounty of shared history. When the Sox opened Fenway Park in 1912, their first opponent in the new park was New York. When Yankee Stadium opened in 1923, the first visitor was Boston. Babe Ruth hit his first professional home run against the Yankees in 1915; Lou Gehrig hit his first against the Red Sox. Boston's Ted Williams played his first game in Yankee Stadium. Roger Maris hit his 61st homer in 1961 off of Boston's Tracy Stallard. When Tom Yawkey bought the Red Sox in 1933, he said he was doing it just so he could beat the Yankees.

Throughout the '40s the hottest debate in baseball concerned who was better, Williams or New York's Joe DiMaggio. In 1941, Williams hit .406, but DiMaggio had a 56-game hitting streak and

BY THE NUMBERS

15

Seasons in which the Yankees and Red Sox have finished 1–2 in their league or division. On 12 of those occasions the Yankees came out on top, including in each year from 1998 through 2002.

31.6

Percent of World Series won by either the Yankees or Red Sox since the Fall Classic began in 1903. Boston and New York have won 48 of the 101 (47.5%) American League championships to date.

11

Of the 24 men used in the 1923 World Series by New York were former Red Sox, including former Boston pitcher Babe Ruth.

22

Career home runs that Yankees shortstop Bucky Dent had hit, in six and a quarter seasons in the major leagues, before his seventh-inning, three-run homer off of Boston's Mike Torrez in the one-game playoff to determine the 1978 American League East champion. Dent's homer provided the winning runs in the Yanks' 5–4 victory.

1,882

Regular-season games played between the two teams. The Yankees hold the alltime edge, 1,037 to 845, dating to the franchise's move from Baltimore to New York in 1903.

won the MVP. Six years later, Williams won the triple crown, but DiMaggio pipped him again for the most valuable player trophy. (Baseball legend has it that the two were nearly traded for each other when both were at the peak of their powers in the 1940s, but supposedly the deal fell through at the last minute.)

Williams helped return Boston to the American League elite, but even the Splendid Splinter could not break the Curse of the Bambino. Every time the Red Sox found themselves in a tight race with New York, they came up short. In 1949, the Sox needed to win just one of two games against New York at Yankee Stadium on the final weekend of the season to lock up the AL pennant. They sent a pair of 20-game winners to the hill, Ellis Kinder (23–6) and Mel Parnell (25–7). Naturally, New York swept the two games. Boston lost a 4–0 lead in the first game, falling 5–4 when light-hitting Yankees outfielder Johnny Lindell, who had hit five homers to that point, belted a solo shot with two outs in the eighth. New York took the second game, and season finale, 5–3, dashing Boston's hopes once again.

It wasn't the last time Boston's season would end in heartbreaking fashion at the hands of New York. Twenty-nine years later, the Sox led the Yankees by 14 games in mid-July, only to see their cushion deflate and be forced to a one-game playoff against you-know-who. Boston went ahead 2–0 but lost the game when Yankees shortstop Bucky Dent, who was never considered a long-ball threat, knocked one

Carlton Fisk (left, 27) and Thurman Munson met at home plate during a 1977 Red Sox–Yankees clash. Boston won 97 games that year but missed the playoffs because New York won 100.

The 2002 installment of the Ohio State–Michigan rivalry affected the national title chase as the Buckeyes and Craig Krenzel (16) edged the Wolverines 14–9 to preserve their unbeaten season.

over the Green Monster—as Fenway's tall but shallowly placed leftfield fence is nicknamed—with two outs in the seventh. Right around that moment, the early edition of the *Boston Globe* rolled off the presses boasting RED SOX AHEAD. As any Red Sox fan will tell you, "ahead" is a place the Sox rarely—and then only fleetingly—find themselves with respect to the Yankees.

While baseball's best rivalry has been characterized by one-sidedness, college football's greatest annual engagement—between Ohio State and Michigan—has been far more evenly contested but no less heartbreaking, thanks largely to the schedule-maker. The two Big Ten powerhouses have been playing each other on their regular season's final Saturday since 1935. If either team has any designs on winning a title, its last regular-season hurdle will be its fiercest rival.

In 1968, Ohio State kicked off the Michigan game as an undefeated team looking to win its first national championship since 1957. The Buckeyes did not falter at the finish, welcoming Michigan to Columbus and pummelling them 50–14. Shortly thereafter, Wolverines coach Bump Elliott departed. The Buckeyes went on to beat Southern Cal 27–16 in the Rose Bowl to wrap up the national title. Elliott was replaced at Michigan by Bo Schembechler, who was incredibly grumpy for a man who hadn't yet turned 40. Schembechler acquired his cantankerousness at the knee of college football's biggest grump—Ohio State coach Woody Hayes, for whom Schembechler played at Miami of Ohio before serving as one of his top assistants at Ohio State.

These cranky compatriots turned an already simmering rivalry into a rapidly boiling one. (Each of them eventually suffered a heart attack on the job.) In their first head-to-head meeting, in Ann Arbor in '69, Schembechler ended his mentor's 22-game winning streak with a 24–12 upset that knocked the Buckeyes from the No. 1 ranking. Hayes was so livid

that he had a rug made with the final score embroidered on it, so that every time his players walked into or out of the locker room in 1970 they would have to step on it. The motivational ploy worked. When they met in Columbus that season—both were undefeated—the fifth-ranked Buckeyes beat the fourth-ranked Wolverines 20–9. The rivalry went back-and-forth from there. Either Michigan or Ohio State won the Big Ten every year from 1968 to 1977, and in every year but one, the conference title came down to their head-to-head matchup.

Beating Michigan became an obsession for Ohio State fans. In the 1980s and '90s, Buckeyes coach John Cooper amassed a record second only to that of the great Hayes, winning 111 games in 13 years. But Cooper won just twice against Michigan, and on two occasions—1995 and '96—he entered the season's final game undefeated and on the brink of the school's first national championship since that 1968 triumph. Both times he lost—in '95 when Michigan tailback Tim Biakabutuka rushed for 313 yards in a 31–23 upset, and in '96 when Michigan slipped by

Pillars of the fabled Celtic–Rangers rivalry, the most bitter matchup in soccer, have included Rangers' Ally McCoist (right, shooting), who starred in the 1980s, and Celtic's Kenny Dalglish (left 9), a standout from the 1970s.

the Buckeyes for a 13–9 victory on a wet field. Losing to Michigan—despite beating just about everyone else—cost Cooper his job in 2001. "That was a big factor, and the reason I won't be coaching here anymore," Cooper said.

As impressive as Michigan and Ohio State's dominance of the Big Ten is, and as much as each covets victory over the other, that midwest rivalry has nothing on the grudge between Celtic and Rangers, Scotland's top professional soccer teams, who between them have won 87 of the 105 league titles contested since 1890. It's a hackneyed cliché in America that sport is a religion. In Glasgow, though, the industrial city of 700,000 that both teams call home, soccer and religion are deeply entwined. Rangers were founded in 1873 by Scotsmen Peter Campbell, William McBeath, and brothers Moses and Peter McNeil. Celtic was established in 1888 as a social organization to aid the city's poor Catholic, largely Irish, immigrants. The first game between the new

teams kicked off in May of 1888. Celtic won 5–2, and after the game, players from both teams sat down together for supper and a celebration. Things haven't been so friendly since. Celtic became synonymous with Catholic; Rangers with Protestant. The rivalry became heated, and at times mirrored the sectarian violence of Northern Ireland.

And if there's one place into which political correctness has not wended its way in Glasgow, it's the soccer pitch. "It's the last bastion of the sins of our fathers," explained Ian McGarry, a soccer writer for the *Scottish Daily Mail* in 1999. "In the past the division represented itself in the workplace and in everyday society, but now the only place where it's still acceptable is a sporting occasion."

In other words, expressions and gestures that

would be considered unacceptable in other contexts, still find expression in the Old Firm, as the legendary rivalry is known. Rangers (and England) great Paul Gascoigne once celebrated a goal against Celtic by mimicking a flute player, a pointed gesture that infuriated Celtic fans and league officials. Gascoigne's actions were meant as a symbol of William of Orange's victory over the Catholics at the Battle of the Boyne in 1690. Three hundred years later, it still

carried a sting. When Mo Johnston became the first Catholic to sign with Rangers since World War I, it infuriated both sides: Rangers fans burned their scarves and tickets, and Celtic fans sent him death threats.

The rivalry has produced some brilliant soccer, and the teams rank among Europe's elite to this day, but the Old Firm has also been marked by more fights than anyone can remember and scores of

Boston's Bob Cousy (with ball) dazzled the Lakers, who played in Minneapolis at the time, with his passing skills in a 1955 game.

deaths. During a break in the action of a 1961 World Cup qualifying game between Scotland and Czechoslovakia, a fistfight broke out between Scotland teammates Jim Baxter and Pat Crerand over who would get to use the trainer's sponge first. When they weren't trying to help their country qualify for the Cup, Baxter played his club ball for Rangers and Crerand for Celtic.

"It all comes down to Catholics and Protestants," said Pete Rooney, who sold programs at Celtic Park for over half a century. "I hate them, and that won't ever change." Even now, when U.S.–style free agency has opened up British soccer to players from all nations, thereby diluting, if not eliminating, the local flavor of the rivalry, the emnity remains, though the most venomous feelings reside with the supporters, not the players.

One rivalry that did witness a sea change in emotion is the Lakers–Celtics matchup, which reached its heyday in the mid-1980s. It all began in the '60s, though, when Boston beat Los Angeles in the NBA Finals six times. (The Celtics also beat the Minneapolis Lakers in 1959.) The last of those showdowns was the most dramatic. As dominant as the Celtics had been, in the 1968–69 season they were showing their age. Center Bill Russell, their player-coach, was 35, and Sam Jones was 36. Boston went just 48–34, and the Lakers, who added Wilt Chamberlain before the season to do battle with Russell under the boards, went 55–27. That meant that when the teams met in the Finals, Los Angeles would have home court advantage.

They split the first six games, setting up a decisive tilt at the Forum. Perhaps unintentionally tempting fate, Lakers owner Jack Kent Cooke had lined up quite the victory celebration for his team. Balloons hung from the Forum ceiling, the USC band was on hand with sheet music for "Happy Days Are Here Again," and there was plenty of champagne on ice. "Somehow, we got a hold of a script for the Lakers' celebration," said Boston forward John Havlicek. "They had it all planned. We hung it in our locker room."

With Boston leading 103–102 and slightly more than a minute to play, Celtic forward Don Nelson took a jumper that hit the back of the rim and bounced four feet in the air. Up, up, up it went . . . and touched nothing but net on its way back down. The Lakers couldn't bounce back, and Boston won 108–106. "I'll always remember those balloons and that shot, too," said Celtics president Red Auerbach

years later. "That made it more special than all the other titles we won."

As Russell walked out of the locker room, he was stopped by Boston trainer Joe DeLauri, who asked, "Where are you heading, Russ?"

"Joe, I've just played my last game."

And with that, Russell walked out the door, taking the Celtics dynasty with him.

Boston won two titles in the '70s, but they didn't regain their mystique until they gambled and took Indiana State's Larry Bird, who still had one year of school left, with the sixth pick in the 1978 draft. The following year, Los Angeles made Michigan State guard Magic Johnson, who led the Spartans past Bird's Sycamores in the 1979 NCAA title game, the first pick in the draft. That fall, both players entered the league and quickly transformed it into the prosperous, high-profile entity it is today.

Five years later the Lakers and Celtics met in the NBA Finals. Los Angeles had won two titles and Boston had won one in the intervening years, but this was the first time Bird and Magic squared off against each other for the NBA title. The teams flooded the court with future Hall of Famers (each franchise started three of them) and current All-Stars, so to think of the series as strictly Magic vs. Bird is to slight the other great players on the court, but that's the way it was perceived. Pete Newell, who coached Cal to the 1959 NCAA title and was serving as a consultant for the

Golden State Warriors in '85, summed it up, saying, "Oh, they'll say it's not a one-on-one game, and they'll point out that they're not even guarding each other, and you can't blame them for doing that. These are two of the greatest players we've ever had, and even though Magic's a guard and Bird's a forward, they sure as heck realize there are going to be comparisons made. Naturally, they want to be at their best. If you were Raquel Welch and you lived across the street from Marilyn Monroe, you'd make damn sure you looked good every time you went out the front door."

It was a mouth-watering series for fans. In their first five years in the league, Bird and Magic went head-to-head only seven times. (The teams played twice a year, but Magic was hurt for three of the meetings.) Now, fans would see that many games in a two-week span. "It's like the opening of a great play," said Lakers GM Jerry West. "Everybody's waiting to see it."

And the production lived up to its advance notices. The series went seven games, with the Celtics winning the decider, 111–102. Bird averaged 27.4 points and 14 rebounds per game; Johnson scored 18 a game and dished out a Finals–record 95 assists. The following year, the rivalry acquired an edge, as great rivalries are prone to do. Boston forward Kevin McHale jousted with Lakers coach Pat Riley in the press, contrasting the Celtics' "longshoremen" with the Lakers' "movie stars." And the teams did more than talk trash. In Game 3, Bird started a pileup that looked like a rugby scrum, with Los Angeles forward Kurt Rambis—the Lakers' lone longshoreman—diving in. (Boston radio announcer Johnny Most likened Rambis to a creature "from a sewer" who perhaps should be "kicked out of the league.") There were two other skirmishes in the game, both involving McHale. "We should meet them out in the parking lot and have a fight to get it out of our system," Bird said. "I don't know if the league is up for it, but the Celtics are."

Magic (with ball) and Bird picked up where Russell and Chamberlain left off, adding another storied chapter to a classic rivalry.

The league most certainly was not up for it. Before Game 4, NBA vice president for operations Scotty Stirling warned the opposing coaches, Riley and K.C. Jones, that the kind of horseplay seen in Games 2 and 3 would be dealt with swiftly and severely if it should happen again. The teams behaved, for the most part, during the rest of the series, and Los Angeles flew in the face of years of history to become the first team to beat the Celtics in a seventh game on the hallowed parquet floor of Boston Garden.

The Lakers won what turned out to be the rubber match in '87, a Finals in which Kareem Abdul-Jabbar punched Boston's Greg Kite in the face in Game 4. The next year, some even rougher types, the notorious bad-boy Detroit Pistons, ascended in the Eastern Conference, and the Lakers and Celtics haven't met in the Finals since. "The most fun I had playing basketball was playing against the Los Angeles Lakers," Bird said. "That's what basketball is all about. When a Boston Celtic gets defeated by a Los Angeles Laker, if you're competitive and have a desire to win, you get this sickness in your gut . . . the worst feeling you could ever have. I can remember flying home on our flight and being so disgusted, I could care less if the plane crashed or not."

"Hate is a heavy word, but, yeah, you hated them," Johnson said. "You almost had to hate the Celtics when you were playing against them, because you got to conjure up everything in your body to go out there and play against the Celtics and Larry."

But through it all, Johnson and Bird developed at first a healthy respect for one another, and then a close friendship. When Johnson was inducted into the Basketball Hall of Fame in 2002, he was presented by Bird. "I was going to write a big speech because I wanted to talk from my heart, but I said, 'Damn, he broke my heart so many times, do I have anything left?' " Bird said.

For his part, Magic simply said, "There's never been basketball like the Lakers and Celtics played. Never. And I don't know if there ever will be." —M.B.

No fewer than six rows of seats, two of them occupied by stadium security officers, were required to keep Rangers fans (far right) sufficiently separated from their Celtic rivals during the May 1999 meeting between the two archrivals at Celtic Park. With U.S. captain Claudio Reyna in midfield, Rangers won the game 3–0 and clinched the Scottish Premier League title with the victory, marking the first time in 334 Old Firm meetings that they wrapped up the season title on Celtic turf.

E20

165

Tempers flared during a 1969 game between the Yankees and the Red Sox at Fenway Park after New York outfielder Bobby Murcer (left, being restrained by Thurman Munson [15] and George Scott) was tagged out at the plate by Red Sox catcher Tom Satriano (4). Boston's Ken Brett (center) and Carl Yastrzemski also joined the fray.

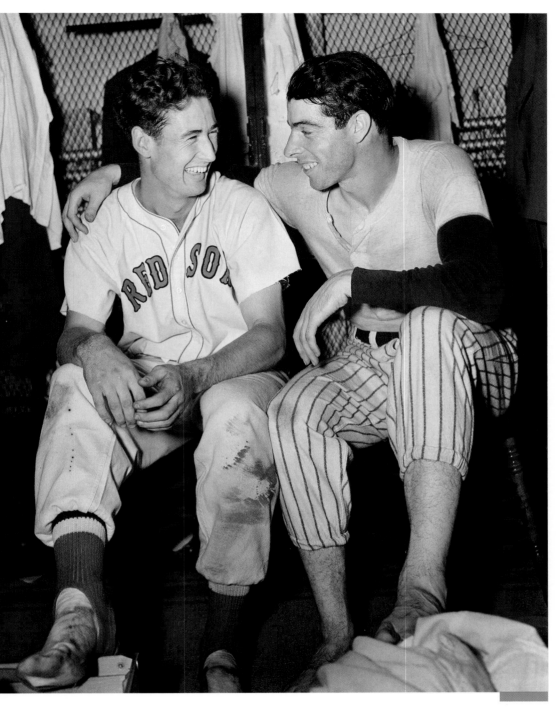

Red Sox icon Williams (above left) joked with legendary Yankee DiMaggio after the All-Star Game in 1941, a highlight year for both players. Williams won the All-Star Game for the American League with a walk-off two-run homer, then went on to hit .406 for the season, while DiMaggio amassed his record 56-game hitting streak, won another World Series ring and was named AL MVP.

On September 7, 1978, Reggie Jackson (left, batting) and the Yankees traveled to Boston for a four-game series with catcher Carlton Fisk and the Red Sox, who led the Yanks by four games in the American League East division at the time. The Yankees set the tone in the first game, routing the Sox 15–3, and went on to a four-game sweep, thereafter referred to in baseball lore as the "Boston Massacre." New York would go on to win the division in a playoff on Oct. 2, when Bucky Dent hit his famous home run at Fenway.

The Lakers–Celtics rivalry is studded with Hall of Fame players, including the Lakers' Jerry West (above, 44) and Boston's John Havlicek (17) and Russell (6), who battled in the 1965 NBA Finals. The Celtics won the series in five games to secure their seventh straight championship, and they would down L.A. for the 1966 title as well.

During a 1991 regular-season game in Los Angeles, Johnson (right, 32) zipped one of his patented no-look passes past Boston's Ed Pinckney (54) as Celtics center Robert Parish (00) trailed the play. Johnson, Bird and Parish were approaching retirement by '91, and the fabled Boston–Los Angeles rivalry awaited a new generation of stars to write its next chapter.

Michigan's Mike Keller (90) and Barry Pierson (29) stopped Rex Kern of Ohio State during the 1969 edition of the teams' annual season-ending grudge match. Michigan won the game 24–12, ending the Buckeyes' 22-game winning streak and knocking them from the top spot in the national polls.

Rangers defender Arthur Numan (above right) brought down Celtic striker John Hartson in the box during the 2002 Scottish Cup Final, prompting cries for a penalty kick from the Celtic faithful. The referee made no call, though, and Rangers went on to score in the last minute to win the game 3–2.